ROBERT L.

EOLOGY AND PASTORAL CARE

Don S. Browning, editor

Pastoral Care
and the
Jewish
Tradition

THEOLOGY AND PASTORAL CARE SERIES

edited by
Don S. Browning

Life Cycle Theory and Pastoral Care
by Donald Capps

Religious Ethics and Pastoral Care
by Don S. Browning

A Roman Catholic Theology of Pastoral Care
by Regis A. Duffy, O.F.M.

The Family and Pastoral Care
by Herbert Anderson

Care of Souls in the Classic Tradition
by Thomas C. Oden

Pastoral Care and Hermeneutics
by Donald Capps

Pastoral Care and the Jewish Tradition
by Robert L. Katz

ROBERT L. KATZ

Pastoral Care and the Jewish Tradition

Empathic Process and Religious Counseling

Don S. Browning, *editor*

THEOLOGY AND PASTORAL CARE

FORTRESS PRESS
PHILADELPHIA

I am grateful to the following for permission to quote from works in which they hold the copyright: Alastair V. Campbell for his *Rediscovering Pastoral Care* (Philadelphia: Westminster Press, 1981); Oxford University Press, publishers of *Theology in the Responsa* by Louis Jacobs (New York and London, 1975); Random House, publishers of *Souls on Fire: Portraits and Legends of Hasidic Masters* by Elie Wiesel (New York, 1978); Yale University Press for *Psychoanalysis and Religion* by Erich Fromm (New Haven, 1950); Fran Liebman for *Peace of Mind* by Joshua Loth Liebman (New York: Simon & Schuster, copyright renewed 1973); and Sylvia Heschel and Farrar, Straus, and Giroux for *A Passion for Truth* by Abraham Joshua Heschel (New York, 1973).

Library of Congress Cataloging in Publication Data

Katz, Robert L.
   Pastoral care and the Jewish tradition.

   (Theology and pastoral care series)
   1. Pastoral counseling (Judaism)   2. Ethics, Jewish.
I. Title. II. Series.
BM652.5.K37 1984   296.6'1   84–47925
ISBN 0–8006–1731–2

To the memory of my son
Michael
June 27, 1954–July 2, 1984

לזכר בני

הנחמד

מיכאל

המכנה

Mickey

שלום על עפרו

Contents

Series Foreword

Our purpose in the Theology and Pastoral Care Series is to present ministers and church leaders with a series of readable books that will (1) retrieve the theological and ethical foundations of the Judeo-Christian tradition for pastoral care, (2) develop lines of communication between pastoral theology and the other disciplines of theology, (3) create an ecumenical dialogue on pastoral care, and (4) do this in such a way as to affirm yet go beyond the recent preoccupation of pastoral care with secular psychotherapy and the other social sciences.

The books in this series are written by authors who are well acquainted with psychology, psychotherapy, and the other social sciences. All of the authors affirm the importance of these disciplines for modern societies and for ministry in particular, but they see them also as potentially destructive of human values unless they are guided in their practical application by tested religious and ethical traditions. But to retrieve the best of the Judeo-Christian tradition for the church's care and counseling is a challenging intellectual task—a task to which few writers in the area of pastoral care have attended with sufficient thoroughness. This series addresses that task out of a broad ecumenical stance, with all of the authors taking an ecumenical approach to theology. Besides a vigorous investigation of Protestant resources, there are specific treatments of pastoral care in Judaism and Catholicism.

We hope that the series will help ministers and church leaders view afresh the theological and ethical foundations of care and counseling. All of the books have a practical dimension, but even more important than that, they help us see care and counseling differently. Compared with writings of the last thirty years in this field, some of the books will seem startlingly different. They will need to be read and pondered with care. But I have little doubt that the series will make a profound and lasting impact upon the way we understand and practice our care for one another.

In this book, Robert L. Katz has given to both Jewish and Christian readers one of the few accounts available on the tradition of pastoral care in Judaism, especially as this tradition has interacted with modern psychology in the twentieth century. Of course, this will be of immediate interest to rabbis and Jewish lay people. But it should also be of interest to the Christian reader as well. It is my conviction that Christians in the twentieth century have misperceived their relation to Judaism. Christian theologians and biblical scholars are now busily at work reconstructing our understanding of that relation. This is one of the most exciting dimensions of contemporary theological scholarship.

But understanding the proper relation of Christianity and Judaism is not just a task for the theologian and biblical scholar. It needs to be pursued at all the levels of these respective traditions, even the more practical levels of pastoral theology and pastoral care. Katz quickly reminds us that Judaism has had no tradition of pastoral care analogous to what can be found in Protestantism or Catholicism. Nonetheless, the rabbi and faithful Jew were expected to visit the sick, care for the bereaved, and help order the practical life of the Jewish community in the areas of marriage, sexuality, death, parent-child relations, etc. Here the rabbi's role as interpreter of the law becomes an exceptionally prominent part of the care of souls in Judaism.

Professor Katz, a member of the faculty at Hebrew Union College, is interested in both preserving and reinterpreting that tradition. He is clearly interested in introducing within the Jewish religious tradition a stronger appreciation for the role of empathic understanding, taken in part from the ethos of modern psychology, as a moderating note within what he feels is an excessive commitment to a certain style of moral rationality. At the same time, he wants to retain an appreciation for this tradition of practical moral rationality as an aspect of the care of souls.

Professor Katz's book comes at an important time, especially for the Christian reader. It comes at a time when the Christian tradition of pastoral care is undergoing a reevaluation of the role of ethics and a moral context in its work. It also comes at a time when both religious traditions are taking each other with new seriousness. Professor Katz has been in intimate contact for years with most of the leaders of the pastoral care movement in both Protestantism and Catholicism. In addition, he is widely acquainted with secular psychotherapy and psychology. He comes to his task in this book with a wealth of experience and relationships. The maturity of his perspective plus his wide familiarity with a fascinating literature full of richly human and charming stories makes it possible for him to communicate an enchanting world of religious meaning and practical wisdom to all his readers, regardless of their religious orientation.

Acknowledgments

I want to thank Professor Don S. Browning for inviting me to write this book and for his patience and support. In important ways, my book is a response to the challenge he gave me. Special thanks go also to Dr. Alfred Gottschalk, President of the Hebrew Union College—Jewish Institute of Religion, for graciously encouraging this effort.

I am also indebted to several colleagues, some of whom were my teachers and others of whom were my students. I mention in particular Dr. Alexander Guttmann, Dr. Ben Zion Wacholder, Dr. Jakob J. Petuchowski, Dr. Richard S. Sarason, and Dr. Barry S. Kogan. My wife, Mimi, and my daughter, Amy Jean, provided editorial advice which I almost always accepted. Such chastisements as they gave were "chastisements of love." My sons, Michael and Jonathan, stood by faithfully, their smiling encouragement and approval affectionately given. I express my gratitude to Louise Selm, caring and disciplined scribe. Miriam November helped me set the project in motion. Betty Brady typed and retyped revisions cheerfully and competently. I want also to express appreciation to Betty Finklestein for her continuous support. Finally, my thanks go to my students, now colleagues and rabbis, with whom I have studied for more than three decades.

I have addressed this book to general readers, introducing themes easily enhanced and extended by following up on the footnotes and on items mentioned in the bibliography. Unless otherwise indicated, translations by the Soncino Press of London have been used for the Babylonian Talmud and for the Midrash Rabbah. Soncino translations—for those wishing to dip a bit more deeply in the "sea of the Talmud"—provide access to original sources. More is gained than is lost through translation.

Introduction

The following story was told about the Kotzker Rebbe (1787–1859), whom a Hasid once consulted about obsessive rumination:

> Once a Hasid came to Reb Mendl with a problem.
> "Rebbe, I have terrible thoughts."
> "Well?"
> "I am afraid to utter them. I am appalled to have such thoughts. Even Hell could not atone for them," the Hasid continued.
> "Out with it."
> "What a wretch I am. Sometimes I think there is neither judgment nor Judge, that the world is lawless, God forbid."
> "Why does it bother you so?" asked the Rebbe.
> "Why?" shouted the Hasid. "If there is no judgment and no Judge, what purpose is there to the whole world?"
> "If the world has no purpose, what concern is it of yours?"
> "Rebbe, if the world has no purpose, of what use is the Torah?"
> "Why should it bother you if the Torah is of no use?"
> "Woe is me, Rebbe. If the Torah is of no use, then all of life is meaningless! That troubles me enormously."
> Reb Mendl replied, "Since you are so deeply concerned, you must be an honest man, and an honest man is permitted to harbor such thoughts."[1]

This is an example of rabbinical counseling by a leader in the mystic movement known as Hasidism (1750 to the present). Even though it may seem far from the methods of today's counselors, who would not approve of the authoritarianism and severity of the Hasidic master, it is of contemporary interest. The Kotzker

Rebbe had no question about the power he believed he had. This faith was shared by the agitated Hasid who came to him to get relief from his guilt and anxiety. We are left with the impression that the client went away satisfied.

Looking at the flow of the interview, we can be impressed with the technique of the Rebbe in checking out the feelings of his counselee. The dialogue was orchestrated to provide the counselor with an accurate understanding of the inner world of his client. The Kotzker Rebbe's diagnostic powers come through clearly, and we can appreciate his intuitive grasp of what people think and feel. The Rebbe did not intervene early to give facile reassurance. He withheld his confirming and supportive statement until his interviewing had clarified certain facts and feelings.

At first he denied the Hasid easy gratification. His aggressive, confrontational style seemed to exacerbate his client's anxiety. Ultimately, the Kotzker Rebbe acted with total confidence in his power to validate his client as a good Jew. The Rebbe used his charismatic authority effectively, but not before he had identified a certain strength and integrity within the Hasid. The sense of commitment that became evident during the interrogation could then be recognized and appreciated by the Hasid. There *was* something he cared about—the Torah!

The Kotzker Rebbe then moved to relax the superego of the Hasid. He gave sanction to the counselee's disturbing thoughts, undoing the compulsive power of the Hasid's ruminations. The disturbing thoughts no longer flooded his consciousness. Guilt was dissipated. When the Hasid left the encounter, he felt himself confirmed in his own worth as a Jew of good character. A wise counselor had intervened to give him an experience that represents one kind of "Jewish" counseling.

Legal power, psychological intuition, suggestion, magic, and charisma were blended in the Hasidic masters. Actually, in ways that seem to clash with classic Judaism, they acted as intercessors between God and man. They dispensed cures, advice, and prescriptions for redemption. Some of the Hasidic masters abused the power of their office. *Zaddikism,* the cult of the *zaddikim,* or holy men, marked the occasional degeneration of Hasidic spirituality. Still, the Hasidic movement continues to flourish today. The tradition of leadership by a few charismatic personalities continues. Hasidic counseling by rebbes is offered to people who want to maintain or to recover a traditional way of religious living, as well as to individuals and families seeking help with marital, parent-child, and other personal problems.

One of the themes in this book is the rich storehouse of psychological insights implicit in Jewish traditions, laws, and legends as well as in certain spiritual movements such as the *musar* movement and Hasidism. Another theme is the process of personal growth and change as seen from the perspectives of psychology and Judaism. The major theme is empathy as a value as well as a method of communication and counseling. And we shall return more than once to the question of whether rabbis should assume their function to be "therapists" or whether it is more authentic and appropriate for rabbis to counsel only as part of their master-role as religious teachers.

Believing that a clear and sound conceptual framework is sure to have practical consequences in face-to-face encounters, we will focus on Jewish attitudes toward counseling and their effect on techniques which, in themselves, are clinical rather than theological. We intend to single out certain themes that have received a special emphasis in Judaism and that could shape rabbinical approaches to counseling. One example of such a theological posture would be the persistent although minor theme in Judaism of man's challenging God. At appropriate moments, these rabbinical counselors, sensitive to this theme, would not discourage protest against God and fate. They could empathize with the need of individuals to groan under the burden of their rage and pain.

Jewish conceptions of human nature will also inform our discussion. Although it is tempting to compare Judaism and dynamic psychology in discussing the nature of the soul, space permits only incidental comments. Nowhere is it our intention to claim that Judaism has anticipated every discovery of psychology or psychotherapy. Rabbis, sure of their identity as religious counselors, can only enhance their effectiveness by selectively applying tested principles of counseling and psychotherapy.

Theology is a venerable discipline, while psychotherapy is exciting, contemporary, and ever so seductive. A great amount of vigilance is necessary for clergy to avoid taking on the therapeutic role. When they do that, religious counselors abdicate their uniqueness. In chapter 5, we shall return to this theme.

COUNSELING IN THE JEWISH COMMUNITY TODAY

Interest in rabbinical counseling has been developing rapidly only since World War II. Rabbis of all groupings allocate time for personal interviewing. Some feel it is intrusive and do it reluctantly; a few welcome it. Only a very small number make it the focus of their rabbinate.

A serious, conscious, and direct concern with the counseling role has been slow to develop. We Jews have not experienced a strong push toward the pastoral counseling movement as in the case of the Christian community. Relatively few rabbis have taken clinical pastoral training, although more of them now enroll in counseling practice and in programs in social work, clinical psychology, and family therapy.

Several reasons may explain the late emergence of a counseling emphasis among rabbis. Unlike Christian pastors, we have not had the model of Jesus the Good Shepherd, the Pastor. It is not in the nature of Judaism to enshrine a single personality as the focus of theology. Among Jews it is the Torah, containing the essence of our faith, that is central, energizing, and formative. In place of a charismatic person to emulate, Jews follow the principle of *imitatio Dei;* to emulate God is incumbent on all Jews, lay or rabbinic.

Furthermore, until recently, we Jews have failed to deal with the theology of counseling. Although the great Hasidic masters who established the institution of the *yichud*—the personal, face-to-face encounter of the master and the disciple—could be said to have anticipated the practice of combining spiritual guidance and therapy, the rabbinate traditionally was identified with teaching, judging, interpreting the Torah, and pursuing scholarship. Nevertheless, Judaism, as will be observed, always addressed the needs of the soul, profoundly and sensitively.

WHAT IS EXPECTED

Now, people expect the rabbi to be a counselor concerned with the inner life of the individual and available for personal meetings about issues in family life, parent-child relations, and problems with a personal faith where more than instruction in Judaism is desired. People expect rabbis to be competent in interviewing, to appreciate the dynamics of the emotional life, and at the very least to be available as a consultant in personal and family crises. Even those commandments, or *mitzvot,* concerned with visiting the sick and counseling the bereaved, which were traditionally incumbent on all Jews, are now seen as "rabbinical": In fact, these commandments are seen as specialized professional obligations of rabbis as they minister to their congregations. Even if rabbis have only a minimal interest in counseling, they are aware that their congregants expect them to fill this role.

Why do congregations now expect their rabbis to do more counseling? One reason is that the example of the Christian clergyman has not escaped the attention of contemporary Jews. Another factor is a growing psychological awareness in the community, along with an increasing expectation that personal, psychological attention should be available from the rabbi.

Another reason for the growing interest in counseling is the coming of age of American Jews, now trying to find themselves as persons after having accommodated to American culture and life. Judaism has survived the transition from Europe to the United States. Now, two generations after the Holocaust and the founding of the State of Israel, Jews are concerned with the content of their own personal and religious experience; they are interested in going beyond the issues of identity and the problems of Jewish survival, of group preservation. They now ask what Judaism can do for them as persons. Rabbis appreciate this emerging need and are now more ready to address the existential issues they are confronted with in their intimate and direct encounters with individuals of all ages. Rabbis are sensitive to problems in the Jewish family and to important transitions in the life cycle.

Now confronting the rabbi are questions about aging:

> I am tired, old, always in pain, Rabbi. Why can't I put an end to it?

> I am lonely. My children don't visit me. My grandchildren hardly know who I am.

Or questions like these about jobs:

> I am a failure in my profession. I'm a disappointment to my family. I have no self-respect. Rabbi, what shall I do?

> I don't like all this infighting on the job. I have to push myself to keep on selling products people don't really need. I don't believe they're any good myself. Can you help me find something to do working with people and making me feel more useful in the community?

Or questions about family life:

> What's happening to my marriage, Rabbi?

> I'm not married, but I'm three months pregnant. I want to keep my baby.

> My daughter has run away to join the Moonies. How can I get her back, Rabbi?

> Rabbi, you officiated at our marriage. My husband just moved out—what can I do?

> My son is going to be bar mitzvahed, and my former wife keeps arguing that her new husband should have a part in the ceremony and stand on the pulpit with us. I won't have it, Rabbi!

Or a question about religious belief:

Why is my child going to die like this? I thought cancer struck only old people. Why does God do this to such an innocent child with so much to live for?

Although not all questions addressed to the rabbi are so urgent and dramatic, a great many involve difficulties in living and problems with personal faith, morality, and identity. People anticipate that rabbis will be a resource and count on them to be accessible and to be interested in their existential questions.

HOW RABBIS RESPOND

Rabbis often feel they have to choose between taking the role of *mocheach,* moral judge, or the role of *menahem,* giver of care, consoler. Some rabbis avoid both, preferring the role of *talmid chacham,* or disciple of the wise, objective teacher and guide—an honored role in the history of the rabbinate. They may be concerned more with principle and less with the personal consequences of the choices their congregants make.

At such junctures some rabbis will make pronouncements as though wearing the mantle of the *dayyan,* the judge. They may cite the sources, confident that Judaism has a ready answer for the issue at hand, and feel that they are authentic only when expounding the meaning of the text.

Other rabbis will respond empathetically as persons of genuine sensitivity. Because I shall later engage in a fuller discussion of rabbinic empathy, I now make only brief reference to Rabbi Leo Baeck, liberal rabbinical leader of Berlin, who survived Theresienstadt to continue teaching in London and Cincinnati: "To place oneself in the position of our neighbor, to understand his hope and his yearning, to grasp the need of his heart, is the presupposition of all neighborly love, the outcome of our knowledge of his soul."[2] The rabbi can be a resource in the healing of the soul (*refuat hanefesh*) as well as in the fulfillment of the self (*tikkun hanefesh*).

Some rabbis invest their energies in the communitarian aspects of Jewish life, doing counseling only when they cannot avoid it.

For two generations, Jews have been preoccupied with the Holocaust, with the Zionist dream and reality, with problems facing Soviet Jews, and other issues in the survival of the Jewish people.

Rabbi Joshua Loth Liebman, author of the best seller *Peace of Mind,* had been excited by the possibilities of a creative alliance of Judaism and psychoanalysis. He felt obliged to confront the issue of reconciling the possible conflict between counseling and social justice, between personal and group salvation. "Our much heralded society of security will remain a Utopian vision so long as the individuals composing that society are desperately insecure, not only economically but emotionally and spiritually."[3] Liebman was a powerful advocate of the need to search for answers "about the universal human dilemmas of conscience, love, fear, grief, and God": "Men and women have to learn how to understand and manage their feelings of hostility against family rivals and work competitors, their moods of aggression, their reactions of fear in the presence of rejection or defeat."[4] Liebman's chapter entitled "Grief's Slow Wisdom" is a superb illustration of how psychological understanding can enrich and supplement the wisdom inherent in religious insight and practice.

Concern for social justice, although somewhat diminished in the past decade, continues to command the energies and resources of Jewish leaders, lay and rabbinic. While some rabbis do as little counseling as possible because their hearts lie in the causes of community, social justice, Zionism, and Jewish education, others take counseling seriously and want to be effective empathizers, exemplifying in their counseling the concern for personal salvation that has always been one of the major themes of Judaism.

PERSONAL SALVATION

In Lev. 18:5 we read that the purpose of the Torah is to help a person live. The individual life is addressed here. The prophet

Ezekiel spoke to the salvific concerns of the individual: "For I have no pleasure in the death of anyone, says the Lord God; so turn and live" (Ezek. 18:32). The Ten Commandments are addressed to individuals. In the Hebrew, "you" is in the singular— "You" shall not commit adultery, and so with the other commandments.

The psalms, also concerned with the individual, include magnificent evocations of human loneliness, of despair, and of the yearning for salvation:

> I lie awake; I am like a lonely bird on the housetop.
> All the days my enemies taunt me (Ps. 102:7).

> My eye wastes away because of grief,
> it grows weak because of all my foes (Ps. 6:7).

> Lead me in thy truth, and teach me,
> for thou art the God of my salvation;
> for thee I wait all the day long (Ps. 25:5).

> There is no soundness in my flesh
> because of thy indignation;
> there is no health in my bones
> because of my sin (Ps. 38:3).

> My soul thirsts for God,
> for the living God (42:2).

The Book of Proverbs abounds in practical counsel for individuals. It also addresses the needs of the psyche:

> Hope deferred makes the heart sick (Prov. 13:12).

> Who can say, "I have made my heart clean;
> I am pure from my sin?" (Prov. 20:9).

> Do you see a man who is wise in his own eyes?
> There is more hope for a fool than for him (Prov. 26:12).

Note that it is the individual who speaks. These words from Psalms and Proverbs address issues in the psyche. The Mishnah, particularly the tractate Avoth, from which we shall quote frequently, also speaks directly to persons. Its ethical admonitions address the dilemmas of private existence as well as those of morality:

> In a place where there are no men, strive thou to be a man (2:5).
>
> Let the honor of thy disciple be as dear to thee as thine own (4:12).
>
> Rejoice not when thine enemy falleth and let not thy heart be glad when he stumbleth (4:19).

A famous passage in the Talmud calls attention to what people must do as individuals in order to achieve salvation:

> In the next world, when a man is led in for judgment he is asked, did you deal faithfully, i.e., with integrity, did you fix times for learning, did you engage in procreation, *did you hope for salvation*, did you engage in the dialectic of wisdom, did you understand one thing from another?[5]

If we came to the philosopher Maimonides with our problems, he would guide us to salvation through intellectual enlightenment. The outpouring of ethical literature in the Middle Ages demonstrated a profound Jewish concern for the transformation of individual character. In the nineteenth century, the *musar* movement developed special exercises to help individuals search their souls and confess their sins. We have already mentioned the concern for individuals which was typical of Hasidism.

The new emphasis on counseling in Judaism only resumes and reemphasizes the theme of personal salvation. How we respond to individuals, how we mediate between the moral code of the community and the dilemmas and anxieties of individuals, how rabbis "listen with the heart" to persons in pain—these are the themes in the pages to follow.

Rabbis have not always sensed the connection between the traditional sources and the actual needs of individual Jews. They have proceeded to wholesale the teachings of Judaism without paying attention to questions that agitate the hearts and minds of their contemporaries. It is not just the psychotherapist who re-

minds us of our failures to listen. The philosopher Franz Rosenzweig (1886–1929) once observed that preaching often fails because the partner in conversation is missing. The preacher "re-
sembles the deaf, because he too hears no reply." Rosenzweig's
stricture could apply to the counselor as well as to the preacher:

> The forced and artificial timeliness of the sermon, therefore, has
> always a touch of the outlived, of the antiquated. The preacher acts
> as if he had been asked. But none has asked him. And thus, also from
> the point of view of the content, all he says seems empty.[6]

The philosopher invites us to "listen" and then "words will come
to the listener."

THERAPISTS OR
RELIGIOUS COUNSELORS

Both clergy and psychotherapists pay attention to the psyche,
or soul, of individuals. While they need not replicate each other's
work, they do have common interests. Although most psychotherapists show little disposition to learn anything from the
clergy, we are ready to learn from them when any of their tested
insights can help us in our own work. To learn from
psychotherapists is not to play false to religion or to set up
psychotherapy as the final arbiter of what is good or bad in our
counseling.

We have much to learn from therapists, because they have
nearly a century of clinical experience and research into what
actually happens in the counseling relationship. But therapists
are relatively unsophisticated about philosophic and moral questions. Freud once wrote to his friend, the Rev. Oskar Pfister, "I do
not break my head very much about good and evil, but I have
found little that is 'good' about human beings on the whole."[7]

Still psychotherapists have observed the human psyche persist-
ently and deeply. They strive to get at the truth about what people
really want, how people manipulate themselves and others, and
how people dodge responsibility. Socrates, Job, and Goethe pene-

trated more deeply into human nature and destiny, but Sigmund Freud, Erich Fromm, and Heinz Kohut have taught us self-confrontation.

As rabbis we are not exactly strangers to self-examination. In prayer we practice confession. When we search our hearts in meditation we try to confront our psyche with the greatest possible commitment to truth. Psychotherapy gives us still another modality for soul-searching. It may lead us to deeper levels of self-knowledge and provide us with a different technology for gaining access to parts of our consciousness that often escape our attention.

From psychotherapists we can learn how to wait for the questions to come, how to control our need to rescue, and, putting it bluntly, how to check our impulse to merchandise religion as a salvation package. Clergy, when untrained and impulsive, often turn out to be "futile and inept counselors," like Job's three friends. We know so much truth about man, and we are the guardians of such great messianic hopes, that we can be impatient with those individuals who are not ready to soar with us as we rise to the heights of spirituality, or hope to.

What will be the shape of rabbinical counseling once we add psychological sophistication to the practice of theology? Will a new paradigm of rabbinical counseling emerge in a shape we cannot yet foresee? May we anticipate a new religious specialist who will be teacher cum counselor? Will the emerging rabbi use the small-group method (as in the *Havurah* movement) and follow the model of Los Angeles Rabbi Harold Schulweis, who has written so perceptively about the crisis of faith and morale among contemporary Jews? The frontiers of rabbinical counseling challenge contemporary rabbis to develop new models of counseling and new styles of dialogue that will enhance traditional wisdom with the care and skill of the empathizer.

Rabbis should not feel obliged to abandon the language of tradition as they move closer to accepting the challenge of personal counseling. There is a task here: to rediscover the dimension of counseling within Judaism and to make our own the perceptions and truths Judaism offers about personal salvation. It is not an either/or situation. Joining the ranks of therapists and counselors could lead us to slight the poetry and the universal vision of sources that address the needs of the soul. At the same time, it is true that many who encounter dynamic psychology come away even more impressed by the concern in Judaism's classic sources with issues of personal salvation and of individual moral responsibility.

> Rabbi Baruqa of Huza often went to the market place at Lapet. One day, the Prophet Elijah appeared to him there. Rabbi Baruqa asked him: "Is there anyone among all these people who will have a share in the World-to-Come?"
> Elijah answered: "There is none."
> Later, two men came to the market place; Elijah said to Rabbi Baruqa: "Those two will have a share in the World-to-Come!"
> Rabbi Baruqa asked the newcomers: "What is your occupation?"
> They replied: "We are clowns. When we see someone who is sad, we cheer him up. When we see two people quarreling, we try to make peace between them."[8]

THE VARIETIES OF JUDAISM

To orient the reader I want to comment on the nature of Judaism with its pluralistic traditions and on my own frame of reference as a Reform Rabbi. I shall refer from time to time to "Judaism," to "the classic rabbis," and to the "sources."

Anyone wishing a fuller sampler of "Jewish" theology has only to look at the pages of the Talmud, where every conceivable alternative is considered seriously and where arguments often are amassed in dazzling profusion. There are cases when even the *halacha* (the conclusive decision) is left open. But not everything in classic Judaism is contingent and relative; there are central themes about Jewish ethics and faith.

Rabbis who wish to deepen the religious roots of their counseling can select insights that speak to the need of the day. They will consider the *consequences* for personal experience of Jewish views about instinctual human nature, or the possibility of repenting or changing, or the meaning of love and empathy. We shall turn to those "who searched out the implications [*dorshe reshumot*— preachers] of the Scriptures [and] said, If you wish to know the Creator of the World, learn the *Haggadah:* for from it you will learn to know God and to cleave to His ways."[9]

In the following midrash, we see the rabbis consoling Moses. Moses was bewildered by the arguments and evidence that flowed from Rabbi Akiba and his disciples, who were studying the Torah in the Academy on High. The legend illustrates tradition's awareness of the place of change and development in the history of Judaism.

> Rab Judah said in the name of Rab, When Moses ascended on high he found the Holy One, blessed be He, engaged in affixing coronets to the letters.
>
> Said Moses, "Lord of the Universe, Who stays Thy hand?"
>
> He answered, "There will arise a man, at the end of many genera- tions, Akiba b. Joseph by name, who will expound upon each title heaps and heaps of laws."
>
> "Lord of the Universe," said Moses, "permit me to see him."
>
> He replied, "Turn thee round."
>
> Moses went and sat down behind eight rows [and listened to the discourses on the law]. Not being able to follow their arguments he was ill at ease, but when they came to a certain subject and the disciples said to the master, "Whence do you know it?" and the latter replied, "It is a law given unto Moses at Sinai," he was comforted.[10]

The first two chapters of this book deal with Jewish beliefs concerning the relation of God and human beings and the rela- tionships between people. Chapter 3 highlights turning points in the evolution of rabbinical counseling—sages, mystics, and moralists. Chapter 4 is concerned with the place of values in counseling done by rabbis. The book concludes with a chapter on empathy as the common ground between rabbinical counseling and therapy.

CHAPTER 1

God and Man

When he calls to me, I will answer him;
I will be with him in trouble. (Ps. 91:15)

As one whom his mother comforts,
so will I comfort you. (Isa. 66:13)

It says: *In all their affliction He was afflicted* (Is. LXIII, 9). God said to
Moses: "Do you not realize that I live in trouble just as Israel lives in
trouble? Know from the place whence I speak unto you—from a
thorn-bush—that I am, as it were, a partner in their trouble."
(Exodus Rabbah 2:5)

Judaism may lack an acknowledged pastoral theology, but one
can be inferred from the classic sources. In this chapter we pro-
pose to draw on biblical, Talmudic, and Midrashic texts to illustrate the enduring concern of Judaism with personal salvation.
Our goal is to demonstrate the model of caring for humanity, of
divine love, which undergirds the most fundamental religious
assumptions in the pastoral or rabbinic role in counseling. God's
relation to human beings can be the paradigm for our own empathy with others. The texts can richly inform the sensibility of
contemporary rabbis seeking for roots, for a sense of continuity
with the tradition, and for a feeling of authenticity in their ministry to individuals.

A contemporary Talmudic scholar, David Weiss Halivni, notes
that it was not customary for the classic rabbis to speak frequently

or lightly of the nature of God. In this sense, Jewish theology departs from Christian theology, which finds it easier to speak of God, and of Jesus, in more structured and formal terms. Halivni observes that the sages of the Talmud experienced difficulty in describing God directly and preferred to wrestle with him, and his nature as it were, on the safer ground of exegesis in the arena of the Torah. Halivni notes that the gentleman of the Talmud "does not air out his existentialist problems with God in public."[1]

Following the great scholar Solomon Schechter, who observed that the rabbis could enunciate religious ideas without spinning them out into creed, Max Kadushin still insisted that the master ideas or "value-concepts" of the rabbis had an innate coherence.[2] Kadushin outlined four concepts: God's justice (*middat ha-din*), God's love (or mercy) (*middat ha-rahamim*), Torah, and Israel. Given their two overriding concepts of justice and mercy, it is not surprising that Jewish religious teachings about God and man closely parallel the insights of contemporary psychology respecting human relations. The poets, prophets, and preachers of the past apprehended so many truths of the inner life and were so sensitive to the needs of people for response and for love that they inevitably attributed the qualities of love and mercy to God and exhorted men and women to follow in God's way and, like him, to be loving and merciful.

GOD'S EMPATHY

The rabbis placed a high value on God's empathy with human beings. They dramatized this attribute. They made it powerful, compelling, and luminously clear. For example, in talking about God, the rabbis used the term *hishva*. Translated, this term means that God made himself like, similar, or identical to the persons he was concerned for. They would say, "the Holy One, blessed be He, made himself similar to. . . ." God became involved in the process of achieving the closest harmony between himself and humanity.[3] The rabbis took care to add a disclaimer such as *kivayachol* ("so to speak") because they were uncomfortable with the anthropomorphic language of this image. But classic Judaism reflected people's need to know that God had intimately identified with them. They were consoled when they knew that God was attuned to their needs. People believed that God had fellow feeling for his people.

We do not always appreciate that postbiblical Judaism perceives God as participating directly in the experience of humankind. Biblical scholar Sheldon H. Blank has called this "God's entanglement in the human situation."[4] A rabbinic theologian has described God's empathy:

> Thus, the Rabbinic Jew said that God was his ever constant and never failing redeemer—and he said it because he felt it; he felt that there was a Presence about him which overflowed with unmeasured love for him and his people. It was some such rooted conviction as this which made him declare that the Shechinah accompanied his people in all their pilgrimages, that the Shechinah sustains the sick, that an injury done to a fellow Israelite is an injury done to the Shechinah, that the Shechinah abides in Israel even in the latter's impurity.[5]

God's involvement with people amounts to "the high tragedy of God's own hurt." The nineteenth-century ethicist Moritz Lazarus wrote: "According to rabbinical interpretations, the poet entertained the bold conception that God desires to be united with man in his suffering, desires to suffer with him."[6] Whenever Israel is enslaved, the Divine Spirit is enslaved and will be liberated only when Israel returns from exile. In the meantime, however, God accompanies Israel everywhere as its constant protector. The *Shechinah* embraces the walls and pillars of the Temple and cries out in anguish when the Temple is destroyed. When he is overcome with grief for his children, God retires to a private chamber and weeps for his people.[7]

When the angels were not inclined to visit Abraham while he convalesced from his circumcision, God rebuked them for their fastidiousness and God himself entered the place of blood and impurity. God cares for all rejected creatures; on his altar the persecuted fowl are acceptable as sacrifices. God wishes to serve as a porter for Israel; he will carry people's burdens if they will but unload the weight of their sins on him. So profound is God's love for humanity that in every judgment he wants his mercy to triumph over his wrath. God is portrayed as entreating himself to let his love prevail: "May it be my will that my children accomplish my will."[8]

HOPE

Hope, another theme in classical rabbinic literature, also pertains to clinical theology. The Talmud lists a number of questions that will be put to each person on the day of judgment. We will be asked "Did you hope for salvation?"[9] A theme inseparable from Judaism is messianism. God works through history. When Jewish messianism calls for faith, it is more a promise than a demand. How that hope will be realized, and what the specific conditions of messianic redemption will be, captured the imagination of the rabbis. For our purposes, it is important to see that messianic hope became part of the Jewish character. Over the centuries, this belief has sustained Jews who were trying to make meaning out of apparent chaos, whether in their private lives or when the conscience of an entire community or nation crumbled.

Some psalms reflect despair and depression (e.g., Psalm 137). There is also a recurring note of lamentation in the Jewish prayerbook. The Day of Atonement is designed to evoke anxiety about the potential for salvation. But what is most representative of Judaism is the promise of redemption. Note particularly the Concluding Service, when the congregation, having tasted anxiety, is assured of God's forgiveness. To use the therapeutic idiom, we experience catharsis and integration. We regain our self-esteem and feel ourselves able to love and be loved.

Now, as evening falls, light dawns within us; hope and trust revive. The shadow that darkened our spirit is vanished; and through the passing cloud there breaks, with the last rays of the setting sun, the radiance of Your forgiving peace. We are restored, renewed by Your love. . . .

You have turned my grief into dancing, released me from my anguish, and surrounded me with gladness: O Lord my God, I shall give thanks to You forever.[10]

The High Holy Day liturgy calls our attention to existential dilemmas in the starkest, most unequivocal way. The famous prayer beginning "Let us proclaim the sacred power of this day" reads:

On Rosh Hashana it is written
On Yom Kippur it is sealed . . .
Who shall live and who shall die
Who shall be tranquil and who shall be troubled.[11]

The grim language is not moderated. All of us live under a judgment; none is permitted to live sheltered by illusion.

The Concluding Service of the Day of Atonement builds toward a climax: the redemption symbolized by the metaphor of God turning toward the people assembled at the Temple in Jerusalem and shining love and acceptance on them. The redemption that the High Holy Days are designed to communicate is something that must be sought and reexperienced each year. It is not an irreversible transformation into a person who is reborn with a new heart and spirit. During the year between one Day of Atonement and the next, not everyone will become alienated from God or from fellow men, but the possibility is always there. Another period of soul-searching is called for in the annual spiritual inventory. But such human failure is not seen as a consequence of a corrupt human nature. Instead, should people sin ("miss the target" in the Hebrew), they can always be redeemed if they do penance (teshuvah).

One cannot read the liturgy without seeing the concern that Judaism has with the salvation of the individual. The same concern emerges in rabbinic sources, as in the almost liturgical passage in the Mishnah: "apply thy mind to three things and thou wilt not come into the power of sin: Know whence thou camest and whither thou art going and before whom thou art destined to give an account and a reckoning."[12]

The Adoration Prayer also addresses the theme of salvation, the quest of the individual and the community for a sense of order and for confidence that history moves in a rational design. If we ask whether peace and wholeness can ever be achieved, we are reminded by the prophet that "on that day, the Lord shall be one and his name one." God's unity is a paradigm for personal redemption and for the integration experienced when the divided, fragmented self coheres. In their everyday prayers, Jews are reminded of the theme of hope, of messianic fulfillment. In the words of the Kaddish,

> May His kingdom soon prevail, in our day,
> in our own lives, and in the life of all Israel.

Petitions for ultimate salvation in no way reflect a mindless, shallow faith. Judaism does not discount the mood of those who have given up hope or joy. "Vanity, vanity, all is vanity"—says Ecclesiastes. Traditionally identified with Solomon, the old preacher, feeling the futility of it all, seems to ask: "Is this all there is?" Later sources probed this issue and in one case revealed a resolution that fails to offer complete consolation.

The schools of Hillel and Shammai, great sages of the early Talmudic period (first century B.C.E.), once engaged in a debate about whether human life has any meaning. They considered the possibility that life is tragic, that the riddle of human existence cannot ever be unraveled. Unsuccessful in finding a solution to the issue, they ultimately were able to agree on charting a course for living the moral life. "They finally took a vote and decided that it were better for man not to have been created, but now that he has been created, let him investigate his past deeds or, as others say, let him examine his future actions."[13] Despite their differences, the rabbis did reach agreement on the affirmation of life itself. The Jewish God is the "living and enduring God." In the great master texts of Judaism, the value of life is taken for granted. In Deut. 30:19, for example, "I call heaven and earth to witness against you this day, that I have set before you life and death, blessing and curse, therefore choose life. . . ." Life and death are choices, yet we are invited and paradoxically almost commanded to choose life.

CALLING GOD TO ACCOUNT

We turn now from describing the elements of the God-man relationship to discussing the encounter itself. Themes of particular significance for the pastoral counselor include confrontation, repentance, and *imitatio Dei*.

In Jewish religious experience, we find that we are on the one hand subject to God's authority but at the same time free to challenge, to confront, and even to negotiate for our rights and our dignity. We accept the omnipotence of God, but we feel free to stand our ground against him, if necessary, and aggressively to stake our claim. The Abraham who submitted to the command to prepare to sacrifice his son is the same Abraham who called God to account in the story of Sodom and Gomorrah. "Shall not the Judge of all earth do justice?" In stating the case for the condemned cities, Abraham confronts God fearlessly, his head unbowed. Another illustration of the individual-versus-God theme is the case of Jacob, in which the aggressive encounter produced a transformation of Jacob's character. When he fought with the angel of God through the night and eventually prevailed, he achieved spiritual greatness. Jacob the deceiver became Israel, the wrestler with God who bargains for the blessings of heaven. Familiar too is the story of Moses, who in his last days attempted to negotiate with God for an extension of his life. In the midrashic sources, we can follow the course of his almost pathetic attempts to face up to God. He cajoles, manipulates, piles argument on argument—all to contravene God's decision.

In the case of Job, we have an elegant and sophisticated confrontation with God. His challenge, bold and relentless, was more than his advisors, Bildad, Zophar, and Eliphaz, could tolerate. But these long-winded counselors, whom Job felt were "breaking him in pieces with words" (Job 19:2), failed to restrain him. With great dignity and stature, Job rejected the option of surrendering without first questioning the mind of God. Job's cry is the cry of every man against pointless tragedy.

> Behold, I cry out, "Violence!" but I am not answered;
> I call aloud but there is no justice. . . .
> He breaks me down on every side,
> and I am gone,
> and my hope has he pulled up like a tree. (Job 19:7, 10)

If we were to rewrite the protocol, what would we say? Would we, as counselors, improve on the theodicy of Job's counselors? Would we offer more cogent arguments? At the least, we would consider listening to him more actively. With all the dignity at his command, Job insisted on a hearing. He asked not that his suffering be mitigated but that he be given a defensible account of why this suffering was imposed on him. If he felt despair, it was because he believed that there had to be a reason behind his tragedy and that God was withholding it from him.

The editors of the Book of Job really do not allow Job to maintain his dignity or his self-esteem. Despite this, at the end he attains new insight.

> I had heard of thee by the hearing of the ear,
> but now my eye sees thee;
> therefore I despise myself,
> and repent in dust and ashes. (Job 42:5-6)

To counselors committed to strong self-esteem as an indicator of emotional integration, the second half of this passage is not congenial. Job the challenger of God stands straighter than Job the masochistic, self-rejecting believer.

The theme of confrontation with God resonates throughout

postbiblical literature. Adding more examples is not necessary. It is only a matter of highlighting certain trends in the history of the Jewish religious experience which might be of interest to the pastoral counselor.

Many sources in Judaism reflect a stance of quietism. The religious life is not always one of strenuous self-assertion and activist protest. We take that for granted. It is perhaps the more familiar religious posture. In bereavement, for example, acceptance is encouraged as an appropriate sign of psychological maturity. But if we as counselors are concerned about fostering individuation and self-esteem, we should not overlook a distinct emphasis in Judaism on the risks of adjusting and conforming too quickly. The model of Job's counselors is too much with us. Do pastoral counselors, and many secular therapists, encourage escapism and compromise with conscience? Do we sanction passivity? It is not unusual to find caricatures of ministers and rabbis as apologists for the establishment who can always be counted on to promise "peace of mind."

We would do well to consider the perseverance in postbiblical literature of the theme of confrontation. According to the Talmudic discussion, the rabbis felt free to argue with God even over the meaning of the words of the Torah. No matter that the Torah is the revealed will of God. One rabbi was audacious enough to shout that the very meaning of the text "is not in heaven" (Deut. 30:12). In the disputation in the Talmudic academy, a voice from heaven had been heard proclaiming that the decision should go according to the opinion of one of the rabbis. What then was the meaning of the Deuteronomic statement?

> Rabbi Jeremiah explained: The Torah had already been revealed at Mount Sinai. We, therefore, need not be concerned with further Heavenly Voices. After all, the Sinaitic Torah itself contains the principle that, in legal matters, *the vote of the majority is decisive.* (Exod. 23:2, in the rabbinic interpretation)
> Later, when Rabbi Nathan met the Prophet Elijah, he asked the Prophet, "What did the Holy One, praised be He, do at that hour?"

Elijah replied, "He smiled and said: 'My children have prevailed against Me! My children have prevailed against Me!' "[14]

Another example of confrontation with God is the angry prayer that a German Jewish liturgist, Isaac bar Shalom, wrote in the year 1147:

There is none like you among the dumb,
Keeping silence and being still in the face of those who aggrieve us.
Our foes are many; they rise up against us,
As they take counsel together to revile us.
"Where is your King?" they taunt us.
But we have not forgotten you nor deceived you.
Do not keep silence![15]

Erich Fromm, longtime student of power and authoritarianism, calls our attention to other examples of this theme in Jewish literature:

After Yom Kippur the Berditschever called over a tailor and asked him to relate his argument with God on the day before. The tailor said:
   "I declared to God: You wish me to repent of my sins, but I have committed only minor offenses; I may have kept left-over cloth, or I may have eaten in a non-Jewish home, where I worked, without washing my hands.
   "But Thou, O Lord, hast committed grievous sins: Thou hast taken away babies from their mothers, and mothers from their babies. Let us be quits: mayest Thou forgive me, and I will forgive Thee."
   Said the Berditschever: "Why did you let God off so easily? You might have forced Him to redeem all of Israel."[16]

From the patriarch Abraham to the masters of the Hasidic movement in eighteenth-century Eastern Europe, and even later in Jewish history, the theme of confrontation with God has continued. In the rabbinic Hebrew it is called *chutzpah klapei shemaya* —impertinent and fearless assertion of claims against God. Judaism not only tolerates but even invites catharsis of rage and of pain.

REPENTANCE: THE THEOLOGY OF
PERSONAL GROWTH

Another major emphasis in Judaism is the process of personal growth and change called "repentance," literally, return or inner "turning." This spiritual process is associated with the High Holy Days, the Days of Awe or the Ten Days of Penitence. The overriding theme is that people are never so enmeshed in moral failure that they cannot extract themselves and make a fresh start. In Jewish theology, God is always ready to receive the penitents, even going forward, to meet them on the way (Judah Halevi 1075–1141).

In counseling we speak of insight, growth and maturation; in religion we speak of transformation or spiritual renewal. Religious language, though quaint, is contemporary in meaning. In Judaism, people are given hope not only that they can change by recovering the qualities of character they may have lost, but also that they can achieve even greater levels of personal integration. People can not only recover lost spirituality, they can also discover new dimensions of personal integrity and new capacities for moral growth. In the High Holy Days, especially, messages of forgiveness and reconciliation are implicit; the sense of sin is alleviated, and if restitution has been made for injury to others, atonement can be completed. But there is more here than relief; the push toward *tikkun* (self-perfection) is felt more strongly than before.

There is a whole complex of ideas in Judaism concerning repentance—ideas that have much in common with psychotherapeutic processes, despite different assumptions. We are not dealing here with simple issues of right or wrong, although behind the Day of Atonement is the great theme of social justice. But atonement (at-one-ment) is also exquisitely the holy day of inner transformation, of the relation of man to himself and to God. If worshipers confess and confront their alienation, forgiveness and reconciliation become real possibilities. Jewish tradition has us believe that going through the process of repentance leads to the experience of forgiveness and the joy of redemption.

Although the Day of Atonement can have important psychological consequences, the holy day was hardly intended to be a psychotherapeutic exercise. The liturgists were not psychologists; the paths to holiness, to the experience of God's nearness, were poetry and prayer. But human realities remain unchanged and both psychology and religion have the psyche, the soul, as a common concern.

The theme of individual responsibility for repentance pervades Jewish liturgy. While every encouragement to repent is given, the individual must take the initiative. If people begin the process of repentance, a hand will be stretched to help them. To pursue the analogy with counseling, the person is free to choose, but the counselor supports those choices that would lead to fulfillment, integration, and growth. Much of biblical language and many of the traditional prayers attempt to intimidate worshipers. They are threatened with dire consequences for making the wrong choices. Despite such authoritarianism, however, the process of repentance is ultimately the individual's own responsibility. An example of a more coercive approach is the warning from Malachi (4:5–6) that unless parents and sons voluntarily reconcile themselves, the great day of the Lord will come and the land will be smitten with a curse. Contrast this with the enchanting vision of peace in Zech. 8:4–5: "Old men and old women shall again sit in the streets of Jerusalem, each with staff in hand for very age. And the streets of the city shall be full of boys and girls playing in its streets."

The process of repentance is continuous. People must always seek to mend their souls. Told that he ought to repent one day before he dies, someone asked, "But I don't know the day of my death." The sages commented, "How much the more so should you repent every day, since tomorrow might be the day of your death."

Aware of the ongoing necessity of repentance, the great master

Moses Maimonides suggested psychological shock as a catalyst to achieve it. He explained that the shofar is blown because its strident notes call people to wake up from their trances (literally, "sleep") and repent. The noise is designed to waken "those who forget the truth, the vanity of the day and waste their years in vanity and emptiness which has no profit. Look to your souls." The concern here is not only with overt sin but also with inner states, not only with good deeds but also with removing such internal sins as hatred and jealousy.

And do not think that a man who is penitent is distanced from the virtuous state of the righteous because of the sins and violations he has committed. That is not at all true. He is as loved and as dear to the Creator as if he had never sinned at all. But not only is this so but his reward is even greater. Since having had a taste of sin he put it aside and exercised control over his instinct [to sin]. Our sages said that in the place where the penitents stand, not even the completely righteous may stand. That is to say that their merit is greater than the merit of those who have never sinned because they have more powers of self-restraint.[17]

It might even be said that those who have undergone such personal transformation attain levels of virtue that would not have been accessible to them had they not sinned.

Here the sources approach a radical observation: Spiritual growth requires failure or sin as a precondition. While this point was never taken to be an invitation to sin, with the possible exception of the late Sabbatean cult of Jacob Frank (1726–91) in the Ukraine, it opens the way to fresh thought about the range of moral growth.

This theme is evoked in the writings of the most prominent contemporary Orthodox theologian, Rabbi Joseph Soloveitchik of Boston. He speaks of the "dynamic energy" of sin. Repentant sinners should not really be encouraged to forget their sin, because recalling it can motivate them to achieve constantly higher levels of purity in their souls. Soloveitchik writes, "The energy of sin draws us, so to speak, towards Heaven." He draws on the example of Resh Lakish, one of the most famous penitents mentioned in the Talmud. After leaving the Academy of Scholars to take up a career as a thief, this sage became an even more spiritual personality when he was persuaded by Rabbi Jochanan to repent and to abandon the life of a thief. Truly penitent people do not suppress the memory of their sins; they transfer the energy generated by the impulse to sin into more ethical and useful projects. Repentance can thus lead to a transformation of evil. To support his argument, Rabbi Soloveitchik quotes the Talmudic passage "Great is repentance because it leads to the throne of the Almighty."[18]

Sin, concludes Soloveitchik, can be a step leading to spiritual elevation. To illustrate, he makes an interesting comparison of love and hate, noting that hate is the more dynamic, active emotion. The completely righteous person knows very little of the latent energy of sin. One who has sinned and repented, however, can transfer to higher causes the energies he used to waste by sinning. Arguing eloquently, Soloveitchik demonstrates that repentance is a dynamic process.

> Through sin, one discovers new psychic energies, a reservoir of power, of stubbornness and of passion whose existence he didn't even suspect prior to the time that he sinned. Now he has the capacity to consecrate all of these energies and to direct them towards heaven. The aggessiveness which he experiences does not allow him to be contented with the usual standards that he used in doing good before he had sinned. . . . No I am not another person; I'm not making a new beginning; I am continuing; I sanctify the evil and transform it.[19]

For Soloveitchik, the sinner has extraordinary possibilities for spiritual growth, whereas the unconflicted, conforming citizen has considerably less potential for moral growth.

One common counseling theme is that people need to control their instinctual energies. The Jewish view of repentance suggests that we can achieve mastery of these forces. One objective of the Day of Atonement is to make us aware of an unrelenting urge to act out self-destructive and antisocial impulses. "Who is the hero?" asked the rabbinic masters. "He who controls his *yetzer*, his evil instinct," was their answer.

The rabbis went so far as to state, paradoxically, that the greater the man, the greater his evil inclination. A story is told about no less a dignitary than Abaye (278–338 c.e.), head of the Talmudic academy in Pumpedita (Babylonia).

> He heard a certain man saying to a woman, "Let us arise betimes and go on our way." "I will," said Abaye, "follow them in order to keep them away from transgression," and he followed them for three parasangs across the meadows. When they parted company he heard them say, "Our company is pleasant, the way is long." "If it were I," said Abaye, "I could not have restrained myself," and so went and leaned in deep anguish against a doorpost, when a certain old man came up to him and taught him: The greater the man, the greater his evil inclination.[20]

In the time to come, according to rabbinic teaching, God will destroy the evil instinct before the eyes of both the righteous and the wicked.

> To the righteous it will have the appearance of a towering hill, and to the wicked it will have the appearance of a hair thread. Both the former and the latter will weep; the righteous will weep saying, "How were we able to overcome such a towering hill!" The wicked also will weep saying, "How is it that we were unable to conquer this hair thread!"[21]

Rabbi Arnold Wolf, a contemporary theologian, explains these different perceptions this way:

> The good man will see his enormous capacity for sin ("like a high mountain"); the evil man will discern how little he had to overcome that he could not ("like a lock of hair"). Obviously the "good" man is not less but more capable of sin, if his *yetzer ha-ra* is so much larger.[22]

Similarities between the rabbinic concept of *yetzer* and the Freudian id need not concern us here. The rabbis were always aware of the power of the instincts. They were confident that, with strenuous efforts, everyone can usually control and sublimate them.

IMITATIO DEI

The most fundamental theological foundation for rabbinical counseling can be found in the principle of *imitatio Dei*. To imitate God, who loves everyone, would be to care for everyone also. Every Jew was expected to follow this ideal. Where the Christian pastoral counselor identifies with Jesus, the rabbinical counselor follows the model of the "Holy One, blessed be He."

The classic rabbis often expatiate on the meaning of the commandment "to follow the *Shechinah*.[23] Through a play on the Hebrew term "I shall praise Him," the rabbis made the association "I and He." The text of the rabbinic passage by Abba Saul (mid-second century) reads: "Be thou like Him; just as He is gracious and compassionate, so be thou gracious and compassionate."[24] Jakob Petuchowski comments that while the Hebrew Bible does enumerate other divine attributes, the rabbis were selective about which were to be imitated. "Thus we do not have Rabbinic passages telling us: 'Just as God punishes the wicked, so do thou punish the wicked; just as God is jealous, so be thou jealous, etc.' although such a paradigm could obviously have been constructed."[25]

A fuller statement in the language of the rabbis is in order because the principle of *imitatio Dei* theologically validates the practice of counseling in Judaism, whether done by rabbis or by others.

> Following the Lord and holding fast to Him can, therefore, only mean imitating His qualities.
>
> He clothes the naked, as it is said in Genesis 3:21: "And the Lord God made for Adam and his wife garments of skin, and He clothed them." You, too, should clothe the naked!
>
> The Holy One, praised be He, visited the sick, as it is said in Genesis 18:1: "The Lord appeared to him [Abraham] by the terebinths of Mamre, when he was sitting at the entrance of the tent as the day grew hot." [This happened while Abraham was recuperating from the effects of his circumcision. See Gen. 17:24]. "You, too, should visit the sick!"

The Holy One, praised be He, comforted the mourners, as it is said in Genesis 25:11: "After the death of Abraham, God blessed his son Isaac." You, too, should comfort the mourners!

The Holy One, praised be He, buried the dead, as it is said in Deuteronomy 34:6: "He [the Lord] buried him [Moses] in the valley in the land of Moab." You, too, should bury the dead![26]

According to this fundamental teaching of Judaism, *gemiluth hasadim* (doing acts of grace, love, and kindness) is the profession, or métier, of God; Abraham, the first Jew, embraced the métier of God.

Although sometimes associated with charity and the giving of material things, *gemiluth hasadim* designates a broader commitment to caring love. Beyond *zedakah* (charity), it means the giving of self, demonstrating one's care and loving concern. It can mean consoling one's friends with sympathetic attention. One responds with love, with a measure of the grace of God, to the needs of others. Here we have a transition from a diffuse principle of love to specific encounters in the helping relationship of counseling. When people give support to their friends, they should invoke God's word and spirit. According to the rabbis, religious counseling has ever-increasing value. "Any counsel which is illumined by the word of God will endure forever."[27]

The encounter between person and person contains the ultimate spiritual significance. If you greet your fellow man truly, it is as though you had confronted the face of the *Shechinah*.[28] All discussion of the theology of rabbinical counseling is really an elaboration of this Midrashic insight. Martin Buber's dialogic theory (see Chapter 2) develops this theme as the ground of real meeting between persons.

The rabbinical counselor identifies with the divine attribute of lovingkindness and encourages it in counselees. Abraham, the first Jew, practiced *gemiluth hasadim*, as did the sages of the Talmud and the Hasidic masters. It still informs the counseling of those rabbis today who see themselves in the Jewish tradition.

CHAPTER 2

Between Person and Person

Rise [and] say something with regard to the comforters of the mourners. . . . our brethren, bestowers of lovingkindnesses, sons of bestowers of lovingkindnesses, who hold fast to the covenant of Abraham our father. (Ketubot 8b)

R. Kahana also said on R. Akiba's authority: Beware of one who counsels thee for his own benefit [literally, "in his own way"]. (Sanhedrin 76b)

To be a man means to be a fellow man. . . . By my choice and my duty I must make a reality in life what is already reality through God. . . . The other man is my fellow because God made him such, and yet my deed is to make him a fellow to me! That which is becomes a commandment. (Rabbi Leo Baeck)

If any man saves a single soul, Scripture imputes it to him as though he had saved a whole world. (Sanhedrin 4:5)

GEMILUTH HASADIM

Seward Hiltner once asked me what term we Jews use to sum up the religious basis of rabbinical counseling.[1] The closest approximation I could give is that of love, or *gemiluth hasadim*. Of course, that concept extends far beyond the counseling relationship and it designates justice, mercy, and communal responsibility.

In Judaism we have no specific term comparable to what Christians call pastoral care. Mutual support goes with being a member of the community; "care" is Jewish, not rabbinical. Because "lovingkindness" refers to care for individuals and goes beyond

meeting physical needs and environmental support, lovingkindness can be applied to dialogues between rabbis and those they
would counsel.[2] Lovingkindness is both an attitude and a process:
it is a theological and religious commitment. At the same time
such dialogue is a *mitzvah,* a religious commandment. In applying
the term *mitzvah* to rabbinical counseling, we are defining counseling as helpful and empathic conversation.

Lovingkindness also tells us something about the attitude we
take toward the people we counsel. Our attitude is not manipula-
tive, nor is it therapeutic, if by therapy we mean a more-or-less
value-free relationship between an expert and a client. Pastoral
counseling takes place when two people meet, within a religious
frame of reference and with an awareness of underlying theology, if you will, about the exceptional nature of their encounter.
The extraordinariness of the encounter does not mean it is
superior to the stance of the secular therapist, from a purely
technical or functional aspect. It simply means that for rabbis the
orientation flows from their religious tradition. The social psychologist George H. Mead observed that those who put themselves in the attitude of others for nonexploitative reasons engage
in a fundamentally religious act.

> "The religious attitude" takes you into the immediate inner attitude
> of the other individual; you are identifying yourself with him in so
> far as you are assisting him, helping him, saving his soul, aiding him
> in this world or the world to come—your attitude is that of salvation
> of the individual.[3]

In Judaism, the theme of love or lovingkindness is in Deut. 6:4,
with the commandment to "love the Lord your God with all your
heart, and with all your soul, and with all your might." It is
specifically derived from Lev. 19:18: "You shall love your neighbor as yourself." This love for the other person is linked to your
love for yourself. Would a counselor be able to model love for
others if he did not experience within himself an appreciation of
having been loved and were he not capable of extending love?
The theme of lovingkindness is spelled out further in the

Mishnah. The full passage clarifies how Judaism makes visible and specific the broad mandate of lovingkindness. It is not love that is singled out as a virtue, but the detailed and concrete ways in which love is made real. Observe that the Mishnah passage that discusses lovingkindness also includes specific references to social justice:

> These are the commandments for which no fixed measure is imposed; leaving the corner of the field for the poor, the gift of the firstfruits, the pilgrimage offering at the Sanctuary on three festivals, deeds of lovingkindness and the study of the Torah. These are the commandments, the fruits of which a man enjoys in this life while the principal endures for him through all eternity: honoring one's father and mother, performing deeds of loving kindness, attending the house of study morning and evening, hospitality to wayfarers, visiting the sick, dowering the bride, accompanying the dead to the grave, devotion in prayer, and making peace between man and his fellow; but the study of the Torah is equivalent to them all.[4]

We Jews praise the God who practices lovingkindness. This theme is consistently reiterated in our liturgy. "Thou upholdest the falling, healest the sick, settest free those in bondage." He is the God "who opens the eyes of the blind, clothes the naked, gives strength to the weary." Another passage portrays God as "raising up those who are bowed down" (literally, helping those who are bent under the burden of physical and psychic pain to stand straight again).

If the classic rabbis stressed the theme of lovingkindness, they also focused on the human capacity for tragic moral failure. The polar opposite of lovingkindness is hatred without cause. The rabbis attributed the destruction of Jerusalem to the persistence of senseless hostility among its inhabitants. In the Ethics of the Fathers (2:16), we have Rabbi Joshua's statement that the evil eye and the evil instinct and the *hatred of mankind* drive a person out of the world. Was he alluding to death or to the deprivation of eternal life? He might have been saying that persons consumed by hostility are vulnerable to severe mental illness; being driven out of the world may be a metaphor for being driven out of one's mind.

On the Day of Atonement, we Jews make confession, rehearsing our frailties, expressing our sense of unworthiness and chanting doxologies of sin.

> For the sin which we have committed before Thee,
> By the evil inclination
> By stretching forth the neck in pride
> By sinful meditation of the heart
> By envy
> By causeless hatred
> By hardening our hearts
> By confession of the lips
> By idle gossip. . . .

While Judaism does not downplay the tragic dimension or deny man's potential for self-destructive behavior and hostile interpersonal relations, it continues to emphasize the innate worth of the individual. Rabbis never lost an opportunity to remind their people of their innate dignity as unique creations. Although all persons are created by God from a single design, every person constitutes a unique and precious version of the species. The rabbis were so mindful of every individual's unique worth that they suggested that each person should think of himself or herself as having such surpassing worth as to be able to say, "For my sake alone, the whole world could have been created."

All these themes can inform a rabbi's counseling. They provide models for theologically grounded self-esteem and for loving empathy with others.

LOVINGKINDNESS AND EMPATHY: THE HEART OF RELIGIOUS COUNSELING

[The Rabbi] sat among peasants in a village inn and listened to their conversation. Then he heard how one asked the other, "Do you love me, then?" And the latter answered, "Now, of course, I love you very much." But the first regarded him sadly and reproached him for such words: "How can you say you love me? Do you know, then, my faults [needs]?" And then the other fell silent, and silent they sat facing each other, for there was nothing more to say. He who truly loves knows from the depths of his identity with the other, from the root ground of the other's being he knows where his friend is wanting. This alone is love.[5]

In Chapter 1 when discussing God's empathy with man, we identified the process (described in rabbinic literature) of God's making himself similar to human beings, becoming entangled in the human situation, participating in human sorrows. Our model of empathizing with others follows this divine paradigm of empathy.

In the Mishnaic statement "Do not judge thy fellow man until you have come unto his place" (Avoth 2:5), we find an allusion to empathy. A great liberal leader of German Jewry, Rabbi Leo Baeck (1874–1956), defines empathy this way: "To place oneself in the position of our neighbor, to understand his hope and his yearning, to grasp the need of his heart, is the presupposition of all neighborly love; the outcome is our knowledge of his soul."[6] This splendid statement is all the more useful because it helps us appreciate the psychological dynamics that come into play when we apply the classic Jewish teachings of love to human relations. We appreciate this paradigm more keenly because of the insights into empathy gained from psychotherapy. In the Hasidic tradition (that of the mystic group that flourished in eastern Europe beginning with the eighteenth century and that still survives on the American scene), empathy was explained through the metaphor of the religious teacher who gets down into the pit with the suffering Jew. The saintly empathic teachers made themselves identical with or similar to the people they served by climbing down the ladder of holiness and participating in the experience of those who sinned or those who lost their way and needed to be redeemed. "One who intends to raise his friend from the mire and refuse must himself go down to that mire and refuse, in order to bring him up."[7]

The problems of overidentification did not escape the Hasidic teacher. How could the master save the sinner and also extricate himself? He risked being swamped by the sins of others. Before making his descent into the pit on his mission of rescue and salvation, the religious teacher always remembered to tie a rope around his waist. His lifeline was symbolically the rope of faith. With it, he could haul both the sinner and himself up from the slough of despair. The Hasidic masters could understand the suffering souls of their people because they recognized that they shared the same impulses and had the potential for experiencing degradation and alienation.

We find another parable of empathy in a Hasidic story about a lost prince. Ultimately, the king was able to recover his lost son by resorting to a form of empathy. He sent a number of nobles to search for the prince, without success. Finally, one of the king's messengers devised the scheme of making himself appear to be one of the people with whom the prince was reported to be living. The noble put on the clothing worn by the villagers. By assuming their identity, he was able to come into contact with the prince and finally persuade him to return to the side of his royal father.[8] Religious counselors, like the Hasidic masters, go through a process of a "trial identification," making themselves resemble the other person in their imagination.

Empathy is both a process and an ethical and religious attitude. As a process, it gives us insight into what other persons feel and perceive in their situations. As an attitude, empathy signifies caring and lovingkindness. As empathizers, we embody the principle of brotherly love; we love others *as* ourselves. This can be taken in two ways. We love them as much as we love ourselves, and we love them because *they are as we are.* If we consider what empathy means from the point of view of the counselee, we would say that it provides the feeling of being understood and accepted. "The presence of others who see what we see and hear what we hear assures us of the reality of the world and ourselves."[9]

We think of empathy as an act of imagination or projection. But the principle of empathy is the same whether we take it to be an internal psychological process or describe it as a physical activity. The following Hasidic story, retold by Elie Wiesel, is an example of the use of physical empathy. The author of the tale is Nachman of Bratzlav (1772–1810).

In a distant land, a prince lost his mind and imagined himself a rooster. He sought refuge under the table and lived there, naked, refusing to partake of the royal delicacies served in golden dishes— all he wanted and accepted was grain reserved for the roosters. The king was desperate. He sent for the best physicians, the most famous specialists; all admitted their incompetence. So did the magicians. And the monks, the ascetics, the miracle-makers, all their interventions proved fruitless.

One day an unknown sage presented himself at court. "I think that I could heal the prince," he said shyly. "Will you allow me to try?"

The king consented, and to the surprise of all present, the sage removed his clothes, and joining the prince under the table, began to crow like a rooster.

Suspicious, the prince interrogated him: "Who are you and what are you doing here?"

"And you," replied the sage, "who are you and what are you doing here?"

"Can't you see? I am a rooster!"

"Hmm," said the sage, "how very strange to meet you here!"

"Why strange?" "You mean, you don't see? Really not? You don't see that I'm a rooster just like you?"

The two men became friends and swore never to leave each other.

And then the sage undertook to cure the prince by using himself as example. He started by putting on a shirt. The prince couldn't believe his eyes.

"Are you crazy? Are you forgetting who you are? You really want to be a man?"

"You know," said the sage in a gentle voice, "you mustn't ever believe that a rooster who dresses like a man ceases to be a rooster." The prince had to agree. The next day both dressed in a normal way. The sage sent for some dishes from the palace kitchen.

"Wretch! What are you doing?" protested the prince, frightened in the extreme. "Are you going to eat like them now?"

His friend allayed his fears: "Don't ever think that by eating like a man, at his table, a rooster ceases to be what he is; you mustn't ever believe it is enough for a rooster to behave like a man to become human; you can do anything with man, in his world and even for him, and yet remain the rooster you are."

And the prince was convinced; he resumed his life as a prince.[10]

As religious counselors we take empathy to mean imaginative, not physical role-taking. We need more than our physical senses to give us an appreciation of what others are experiencing. Intimate knowledge of another person calls for an act of unencumbered imagination. As Adam Smith wrote in 1759, "Though our brother is on the rack, as long as we ourselves are at our ease, our senses will never inform us of what he suffers."[11]

In using our imaginations, we run the risk of distorting reality. When our hold on our own identity is tenuous, the boundaries that separate us from others can become blurred. We can project our own needs and wishes on other people. When we do this, all we have is our subjective reality and little, if any, objective knowledge about what other people are actually feeling.

Other risks were also known to the classic rabbis. Once we become empathizers, we may not be able to detach ourselves from others. Moreover, sometimes another person's pain stirs the memory of an earlier pain of our own. If this happens, we begin to console ourselves and our attention is distracted from others, so that we forget the original purpose of the meeting. The classic rabbis called attention to the need for constant self-searching in order to eliminate our own blind spots. Resh Lekish said, "Adorn yourself first and then adorn others" (Sanhedrin 18a and 19a). The sense of "adorn" is "solve your own problems."

If we over-identify with our counselees, we lose our ability to remain separate. Our empathy is then likely to fail. The Talmud deals with countertransference when it discusses the potential for judicial abuses. The Talmudic discussion of the risks of bribery for judges can be transposed into the field of counseling. Consider the error of empathy described by the sage Rab Papa:

> A man should not act as a judge either for one whom he loves or for one whom he hates, for no man can see the guilt of one whom he loves or the merit of one whom he hates. Raba stated: What is the reason for [the prohibition against taking] a gift? Because as soon as a man receives a gift from another, he becomes so well disposed towards him that he becomes like his own person, and no man sees himself in the wrong. What is [the meaning of] *shohad* [bribe]? [*She-hu-had*—he, the recipient, is one with the giver].[12]

The rabbis were realistic about describing our limitations when we try to understand other people. Among the seven things that are hidden from humans, said the rabbis, are the day of death and the day of comfort when people will be relieved of their anxieties, the depth of judgment; and [*people do not know*] *what is in their neighbors' hearts.*

MARTIN BUBER, DIALOGUE, AND EMPATHY

The most influential Jewish social philosopher of modern times was Martin Buber (1878–1965), who wrote perceptively of the relations of people and is known for his theology of dialogue. Buber rejected the term "empathy" because he believed that it designated physical processes rather than the more spiritual and subtle aspects of human communication, yet much of his discussion about "imagining the real" and "moving to the side of the other" defines what we counselors mean by empathy.

Buber wrote about our need to turn fully to one another. The other person becomes fully present to us, and we become fully present to him or her. This turning involves more than feeling, which is no more than an accompaniment to the actual relationship between one person and another.

Readers of *I and Thou* will recall Buber's description of the evocation of the *Thou* when two persons are genuinely open to each other. Buber was, of course, concerned with dialogue as a religious experience, although he deals briefly with the use of dialogue in therapy: "A man can ward off with all his strength the belief that God is there, and he tastes him in the strict sacrament of dialogue."[13] Buber says that to communicate we must participate imaginatively in the inner life of the other, include the experience of the other in our own experience. When we surrender ourselves fully to the other person, we gain as much concrete knowledge as we can. Buber's comment about "a bold swinging into the life of the other" parallels therapists' suggestions for empathic communication; therapists recommend an alternating between empathy and separation. When Buber talks about "inclusion," he has in mind an empathic process permitting us to be at our own side and at the side of the other person simultaneously.

There are limits to empathic involvement. Buber reminds us that however fully present we may be to the other person, we must remain detached. Although the dialogue between counselor and client is mutual, the two cannot merge as one. Moreover, the counselor must always be aware of a disposition to direct his or her counseling without respecting the individuality of others. According to Buber, a relationship with the counselee can be falsified if the counselor "is touched by the desire—in however subtle a form—to dominate or to enjoy his patient, or to treat the latter's wish to be dominated or enjoyed by him other than as a wrong condition needing to be cured."[14]

Later we shall refer to Buber's discussion of guilt, a particularly interesting subject to writers like Don Browning who believe that pastoral counseling should be grounded in a moral context. Buber faults psychoanalysts for dulling the sense of guilt in patients, when he discusses the "Melanie case." We must also note Buber's emphasis on a fully accepting relationship, which includes confirming what the person may be as well as what the person is at the present time. In a debate with Carl Rogers on

April 18, 1957, at the University of Michigan, Buber distinguished between Rogerian acceptance and his own theme of
confirmation. With some people, Buber believed, something
more than acceptance is needed.

> There are cases when I must help him against himself. He wants my
> help against himself. . . . What he wants is a being, not only whom he
> can trust as a man trusts another, but a being that gives him now the
> certitude that "there *is* a soil, there *is* an existence. The world is not
> condemned to deprivation, degeneration, destruction. The world
> *can* be redeemed. *I* can be redeemed because there is this trust." And
> if this is reached, now I can help this man even in his struggle against
> himself. This I can do only if I distinguish between accepting and
> confirming.[15]

MODELS OF JEWISH PIETY

The three spiritual models or religious types that evolved in
classic or rabbinic Judaism will help us appreciate the major
motifs that have informed rabbinical counseling. Throughout
Judaism, both the rabbis and others have been involved in a
religious system of values and priorities made visible as ideal
patterns of character and behavior emerged. We can see counseling, like other religious activities, as an extension or application of
some virtues and ideal traits embodied in these major religious
motifs.

In Judaism, the image of the sage or scholar is overwhelmingly
positive, and his unique worth is constantly being reaffirmed.
However, as we shall see later, the strong emphasis on the *talmid
chacham*—the sage or "disciple of the wise"—can work subtly to
inhibit the fuller empathic communication, imagination and feeling, that is essential to counseling.

The late Louis Ginzberg (1873–1953) coined the phrase
"scholar-saint" to describe the learned rabbi whose behavior was
exemplary. He suggested that the scholar-saint exercised a wide
influence because of the power of his learning and the charisma
of his person. The sage—the *talmid chacham*—as well as two other
spiritual models are fully described in Gershom Scholem's

(1897–1982) splendid article entitled "Three Types of Jewish Piety."[16] The three types are *talmid chacham,* the *tsaddik,* and the *hasid.* The *talmid chacham,* literally "disciple of a sage" or rabbinic scholar, places a supreme value on learning and rationality. His field of concentration is the study of Scripture, of rabbinics, and all that goes by the generic term "Torah." The *talmid chacham* is a student who explicates the meaning of Jewish tradition. He is essentially a distinguished intellectual with a great capacity for study. Learning here means the mastery of the tradition. To quote Scholem:

> It is an ideal towards which you can educate people and develop institutions that might produce it. And it is an ideal that held equally for Jews wherever they lived, be it in Yemen or Russia, in Babylonia or France. Even today the power of this ideal has not been broken, although the last generations have made heavy inroads into the traditional ideals of Jewish life and we are witnessing revolutionary changes, both in Israel and the Diaspora, which affect the basis on which this life was built.[17]

Scholem indicates that the two other types, *tsaddik* and *hasid,* are distinguished less by their intellectual qualifications and more by how they carry out their religious commitments. Judaism evolved a large body of ethical literature that appealed to the average person, who was less qualified in Jewish learning than the *talmid chacham.* The *tsaddik* literally is someone whose integrity is vindicated and fully affirmed. He is someone who perseveres soberly in a strenuous effort to be a man of deeds even more than a man of words. He is rewarded because he tries to achieve moral stature, whether he is a scholar of repute or not. He is the "normal" Jew. Like the *talmid chacham,* the *tsaddik* is rational and judicious. Also, he is concerned with an ordered world, ultimately to be redeemed when humankind learns to follow the Torah.

The *hasid* is an enthusiast. He goes beyond what is required of him. He embodies the trait of God's *hesed* ("grace") which tempers the strict measure of justice. To quote Scholem again, "In rabbinic usage, the term *hasid* never means or implies an attitude of mind alone; it always carries the connotation of practical application of such an attitude."[18] The *hasid* was a radical pietist, an exemplar of pure spirituality. Not everyone can be educated to become such a pietist. On the other hand, anyone can be educated to become a *tsaddik* or the "scholar-saint" described by Ginzberg.

These three models, the *talmid chacham,* the *tsaddik,* and the *hasid,* still survive as a religious typology. How would such types inform the counselor's model of himself? The model of the *talmid chacham* is favored by those who are concerned with their credibility as "scientific" and flawlessly rational professionals. Does it inhibit some of the emotional aspects of empathy? Do such "sages" see themselves, like Maimonides did, as guiding the intellectually perplexed by being their cognitive mentors? In so doing, do they miss the subtleties of communication where the self of the counselee is involved?

We shall be referring back to the preconditions outlined in these two basic chapters. We have established some religious or theological guidelines for the contemporary rabbinical counselor.

Without developing them fully at this point, we note that the contemporary counselor is challenged by such religious concepts as confrontation with God, the always renewable opportunity for personal change (repentance), and the theme of hope symbolized in Jewish messianism.

All too frequently, counselors feel called upon to defend God and to justify Jewish teachings when they meet mourners who berate God for permitting a tragic death to occur. Why, we might ask, should the counselor feel defensive and want to offer arguments proving God's ultimate justice and mercy when there is ample historical justification for another position—the person in pain can protest in anguish and challenge God without any restraint? Does the rabbinic confrontation with God appear too radical and too unconventional for today's liturgy? It is difficult to believe that we have a stronger faith than the classic rabbis, yet they were able to encourage their people to demand justice from God and to rage against heaven.

We often encounter a stubborn resistance to change among the people we counsel. At such times, why do we not draw on the classic concept of repentance? Following any movement, ever so slight, toward change, the possibilities for growth abound.

The themes of messianism and of hope are relevant to any counseling effort. Judaism promises no simple salvation, but at the same time it is rooted in a deep belief that God is the God of life. Historically, Jews have been a people of faith. The theme of existentialist despair and *angst* can be located in Jewish sources, but it is secondary to the overriding conviction that life is good and that man is free to choose the good. Rabbinical counselors can present this theme to disaffected and disillusioned congregants, allow them to respond to it, and sustain an open dialogue about what meaning it can have in their lives.

CHAPTER 3

Sages, Moralists, Mystics: Counseling in the Jewish Tradition

For if he cannot be judged, how can he judge? Be just yourself, before demanding it of others. (Sanhedrin 18a)

A man does not know what is in his neighbor's heart. (Pesahim 54b)

[A wise man] enters not into the midst of the words of his fellow and is not hasty to answer. (Avoth 5:7)

Take the beam from between your eyes. (Baba Bathra 15b)

R. Nathan said: Do not taunt your neighbor with the blemish you yourself have. (Baba Mezia 59b)

"Let not anxiety enter thy heart, for it has slain many a person!" But Solomon said likewise. *Anxiety in the heart of man-yashhenna:* maketh it stoop, as Prov. 12:25, care in the heart of a man boweth it down. R. Ammi and R. Assi [differ in its interpretation]: one rendered it, "Let him banish it from his mind," the other, "Let him relate it to others." (Sanhedrin 100b)

If we were to present a full account of counseling in Judaism, we would have to include references to biblical literature and in particular note the activities of priests, prophets, and seers as healers. We intend to illustrate the ways the rabbis seemed to respond to calls for personal help. We must rely on fragments of their conversations, on anecdotes and sayings. If not the letter, then the spirit of their dialogues can be retrieved. If the insights that emerge are not revolutionary, they do reveal a profound concern for persons.

Such continuity as there may be between contemporary and

earlier models of counseling are likely to be found in the examples provided by the teachers of the Mishnah, the masters of the Talmud, the preachers of the Midrash, the practitioners of healing among the Hasidic rebbes, and the spiritual mentors of the *musar* (moralist) movement.

EXAMPLES OF COUNSELING IN CLASSIC LITERATURE

We begin with one counseling activity—visiting the sick. The commandments associated with this variety of counseling actually were (and are) incumbent on all Jews. Only in recent years, perhaps because of the model of the Protestant and Catholic clergy, have visiting the sick and other such activities come to be considered a special responsibility of rabbis.

The rabbis observed that visiting the sick is a serious obligation. One authority said that one ought to visit the sick person a hundred times a day. Another rabbi said:

> He who visits an invalid takes away a sixtieth part of his pain. They [his colleagues] pointed out an objection to R. Huna; if that is so, could sixty people come in and enable him to go down into the street? He answered them: Sixty could accomplish this, but only if they loved him like themselves. But, in any case, they would afford him relief.[1]

In a dramatic way another rabbinic anecdote underscores the value of visiting the sick. It happened that one of the sages fell ill and no one came to visit him. Then the great Rabbi Akiba (50–135 c.e.) took time to visit the ailing scholar. When the patient recovered, he said, "My master, you have revived me." Upon hearing this moving statement, Rabbi Akiba said, "He who does not visit the sick is like a shedder of blood."[2]

In the following story, a rabbi learns that the ability to relieve the pain of another does not necessarily mean he is able to deal with his own distress. In fact, when healers need healing, they must acknowledge their own dependence on others.

R. Johanan had the misfortune to suffer from gallstones for three
and a half years. Once R. Hanina went to visit him. He said to him:
"How do you feel?" He replied: "My sufferings are worse than I can
bear." He said to him: "Don't speak so, but say 'The faithful God.'"
When the pain was very great he used to say "Faithful God," and
when the pain was greater than he could bear, R. Hanina used to go
to him and utter an incantation which gave him relief. Subsequently
R. Hanina fell ill, and R. Johanan went to see him. He said to him:
"How do you feel?" He replied: "How grievous are my sufferings!"
He said to him: "But surely the reward for them is also great!" He
replied: "Why do you not utter that incantation which you pro-
nounced over me and which gave me relief?" He replied: "When I
was out of trouble I could be a surety for others, but now that I am
myself in trouble do I not require another to be a surety for me?"[3]

Aware of the possibility of extending mourning beyond appropriate limits, the rabbis recommended a regimen that would
provide for controlled compassion. They advised that we mortals
should not try to be more compassionate than God himself.

[Our rabbis taught]: *"Weep ye not for the dead, neither bemoan him"* [that
is], *"Weep not for the dead"* [that is] in excess, *"neither bemoan him—*
beyond measure." How is that [applied]?—Three days for weeping
and seven for lamenting and thirty [to refrain] from cutting the hair
and [donning] pressed clothes; hereafter, the Holy One, blessed be
He, says, "Ye are not more compassionate towards him [the de-
parted] than I."[4]

We might extend this principle of control to include a whole
variety of situations in human relations where conscious discipline is required to avoid overidentification. The rabbis did not
anticipate the discoveries of contemporary psychotherapy by ex-
amining emotional reactions clinically or systematically. Intuitively, however, they did appreciate a very human tendency to
give way to self-defeating overreactions. Another Talmudic story
continues the theme of the dangers of unrestrained emotionality.
A sage is being upbraided for not showing more feeling while
mourning the death of his daughter.

Rabbi Hanina's daughter died, [but] he did not weep for her. Said his wife to him, Hast thou sent out a hen from thy house? [Was she nothing more to you than that?]

[Shall I suffer] two "evils" he retorted, "bereavement and blindness?" [Should I weep so much that I will become blind and experience another blow?]"[5]

Another anecdote comments on the misguided efforts of some who would continue to counsel the bereaved long after the customary year of mourning. It is a mark of gross insensitivity to offer counsel at the wrong time. The rabbis noted the narcissism involved in the zeal to counsel.

Said Rabbi Meir: If one meets another mourner after twelve months and then tenders him words of consolation, to what can he be likened? To [the case of] a man who had his leg broken and healed when a physician said to him, come to me and let me break it and set it [again], to show what a great healer I can be.[6]

The following Talmudic story is a fascinating account of what might have been one of the early dialogues between religion and psychiatry. A doctor is concerned about a patient he is treating for anxiety growing out of an obsession with a young woman. The physician prescribed procedures that would have given the patient the sexual gratification he asked for. But the rabbis interposed fundamental moral considerations and rejected the physician's treatment plan outright.

Rab Judah said in Rab's name: A man once conceived a passion for a certain woman, and his heart was consumed by his burning desire [his life being endangered thereby]. When the doctors were consulted, they said, "His only cure is that she shall submit." Thereupon the sages said: "Let him die rather than that she should yield." Then [said the doctors]: "let her stand nude before him"; [they answered] "sooner let him die." "Then," said the doctors, "let her converse with him from behind a fence." "Let him die," the sages replied, "rather than she should converse with him from behind a fence." Now R. Jacob b. Idi and R. Samuel b. Nahmani dispute therein. One said that she was a married woman; the other that she was unmarried.

Now, this is intelligible on the view that she was a married woman, but on the latter, that she was unmarried, why such severity?—R. Papa said: "Because of the disgrace to her family," R. Aha the son of R. Ika said: "That the daughters of Israel may not be immorally dissolute." Then why not marry her?—Marriage would not assuage his passion, even as R. Isaac said: "Since the destruction of the Temple, sexual pleasure has been taken [from those who practice it lawfully] and given to sinners, as it is written, 'Stolen waters are sweet, and bread eaten in secret is pleasant.'"[7]

The sages refused to relax moral standards in the alleged service of the mental health of the patient. The physician would stop at nothing—even violating the privacy and freedom of the woman—in order to cure his patient. This case exemplifies a totally male-centered point of view. The wishes or needs of the woman are not considered; protecting the good name of her family was the overriding concern.

Historically the rabbis always had to deal with the nitty-gritty of human experience. Here is an example of marital counseling by one of the greatest Talmudic masters, Rabbi Meir (second century). It demonstrates more empathy than was evident in the previous case, involving sexual morality.

Rabbi Meir was in the habit of delivering discourses on Sabbath evenings. Among his listeners there was a certain woman.

Once the discourse took a very long time, and the woman stayed until the end. When she returned home, she found that the light had already gone out. Angrily her husband wanted to know: "Where have you been?"

She replied: "I sat listening to a preacher." Her husband now adjured her, saying: "You are forbidden to enter this house until you have spat in the preacher's face!" She stayed away from home one week, two weeks, three weeks. Finally her neighbors said to her: "Are you still quarreling? Come let us go with you to the preacher."

When Rabbi Meir saw her coming, he was able, through the gift of the Holy Spirit, to understand the whole sequence of events.

He said: "My eye hurts. Is there, perhaps, among you an understanding woman, capable of whispering a charm over my eye?"

Now the woman's neighbors said to her: "If you were to go and spit into his eye, you would be able to annul your husband's adjuration."

The woman went, and sat down in front of Rabbi Meir. But she was afraid of him, and she said, "Rabbi, I really have no experience in whispering charms over eyes."

But the Rabbi said: "Nevertheless, do spit in my face seven times! Then I shall be healed."

She did so.

After that, Rabbi Meir said to the woman: "Go home and tell your husband: 'You demanded of me to spit in the preacher's face once; I have done it seven times!'"

After the woman had left, his disciples said to Rabbi Meir: "Is it proper to let the Torah be brought into such contempt? Could you not simply have asked one of us to whisper a charm over your eye?"

But Rabbi Meir replied: "Is it not fitting for Meir to attempt to imitate his Creator? For Rabbi Ishmael had taught: Great is peace, because the Name of God, though written down in holiness, was, according to the divine commandment [Num. 5:11–31], to be blotted out in water, if only peace could thereby be restored between husband and wife!"[8]

THE SCOPE OF
RABBINICAL COUNSELING

The pages of the Talmud are replete with examples of counseling involving ethical, ritual, and familial matters. Nothing human was alien to the rabbis' interest, as the following anecdote makes clear:

Rabh Huna once reprimanded his son, Rabbah: "Why is it that you are not attending the lectures of Rab Hisda? They say about him that his teaching is very incisive."

His son replied: "Why should I go to him? Whenever I am there, Rab Hisda only speaks of worldly matters. He lectures about the functions of the digestive organs and about other purely physical matters."

But the father said to him: "Rab Hisda speaks of God's creatures, and you call that 'worldly'? Go to him!"[9]

The advice that sages gave touched every aspect of human affairs. Nothing was felt to be beyond the scope of their interest or their powers. As Jacob Neusner indicated, the wisdom of the rabbis even included some mastery of magical knowledge. They knew "how to bless and curse, how to heal and how to ensure one's entry into heaven, how to read signs and omens."[10]

A well-known Talmudic passage stresses the supremacy of reason and wisdom. Prophetic knowledge and insight have been granted preeminently to the sages:

> R. Abdimi from Haifa said: Since the day when the Temple was destroyed, prophecy has been taken from the prophets and given to the wise. Is then a wise man not also a prophet?—What he meant was this: Although it has been taken from the prophets, it has not been taken from the wise. Amemar said: "A wise man is even superior to a prophet."[11]

Neusner makes clear that the sages were more than experts in sacred literature. They viewed themselves as members of a fraternity of moral arbiters. While the judgments and insights they offered were intended to carry out the master themes of the Torah, they introduced opinions that went beyond the revealed texts. According to Neusner, "They too became vehicles of revelation, modes of sanctity, and mediators of salvation."[12]

Rabbinic wisdom was captured and preserved in homily as well as in exegesis. Here is such a homily that combines counseling and theological instruction:

> One day, Rabbi Joshua ben Levi asked the Prophet Elijah: "When will the Messiah come?"
>   Elijah answered: "Go to him and ask him!"
>   Rabbi Joshua wanted to know: "But where is he?"
>   Elijah replied: "At the gates of Rome."
>   "And how shall I recognize him?"
>   "He is sitting among the poor lepers. But, while all the others take off all their bandages at once and put them on again all together, the Messiah takes off his bandages one after the other and puts them on again one after the other. For he thinks that God might call him at any minute to bring redemption, and he, therefore, holds himself in a state of constant preparedness."

Rabbi Joshua went to him, and greeted him: "Peace be upon you, my Master and Teacher!"

And the Messiah replied: "Peace be upon you, son of Levi!"

"When will the Master come?"

"Today!" . . .

Later, Rabbi Joshua complained to the Prophet Elijah: "The Messiah has lied to me. He said that he was coming today; but he did not come."

Elijah answered: "You did not understand him correctly. He was quoting Psalm 95:7 to you: 'Today, if you will but hearken to His voice!'"[13]

RESPONSA

Let us now consider a few examples of the Responsa literature, which are pertinent to any account of the ways the rabbis counseled. The Hebrew term for Responsa is *sheelot utshuvot* ("questions and answers"). Usually these Responsa involved an exchange of letters on matters of law, but often they included opinions on almost every aspect of communal, religious, domestic, and personal life. The earliest of such Responsa date from Talmudic times, but the institution of counseling or advising by correspondence continues today. It is estimated that no less than 250,000 items are now included in a number of scattered compendia. Their central theme is always the same: How should Jews behave—what it is that God would have them do?[14]

The Talmud was the major source used by the respondents. Even though guidance might not always be derived from specific classical sources to cover new situations, it was believed, as Jacobs wrote, "that Judaism, if properly investigated, had an answer to every question, was capable of showing which way was right and which way was wrong in matters of ritual, social and family life, reaction to the Gentile community and communal endeavours."[15] Rabbi Israel Isserlein (1390–1460) counseled a student who hesitated to go abroad and study Torah and act against the will of his father. Rabbi Isserlein's advice was unequivocal:

The obligation to study the Torah takes precedence over honouring parents and since it is proper, as the Rabbis say, that a man should follow his instincts when choosing a teacher, the student is permitted to leave his home in order to study the Torah, even though his father objects.[16]

Sometimes the Responsa deal with legalistic minutiae, yet in the example that follows, a clear spiritual message is conveyed. Meir Eisenstadt (d. 1744) was asked why we say "the God of Abraham, the God of Isaac, and the God of Jacob" and not simply "the God of Abraham, Isaac, and Jacob." Eisenstadt's answer is most persuasive: Don't believe in God merely because your father believed in him; each individual should arrive at his own convictions about the existence of God. "We Jews do not believe merely on the strength of tradition, as do 'the nations of the world.' We reason it out for ourselves and, when we do, we see that any belief except pure monotheism is false."[17] Joseph Hayyim of Baghdad (1835–1909) wrote a psychological Responsum to help a man afflicted with severe phobias. Hayyim prescribed the recitation of the *Shema* (Hear O Israel) with full concentration and, among other things, the wearing of an amulet containing the two divine names found in the *kabbalah* (the mystic literature of the thirteenth and fourteenth centuries).

The process of counseling following the model of the Responsa was carried on in the ghettos of Warsaw and Kovno and even in the death camps of the Nazis. Collections of Responsa that originated in the death camps document the effort of Halachic masters to temper the severity of legal rulings with the empathy and love needed by the captives, who daily faced the possibility of death by incineration.

According to Alexander Guttmann, psychology was always used by rabbis in rendering decisions and writing Responsa, but during the Holocaust it assumed even greater importance. In one case cited by Guttmann, a rabbi was consulted because a survivor of a concentration camp was experiencing deep guilt for what he felt was his failure to save his brother. He suffered pangs of conscience and came to the rabbi for help with survivor guilt. The rabbi responded to a specific case of human despair and depression:

> First, he completely exonerates the man who possibly, if not probably, caused the death of his brother due to negligence. Then, he suggests that since there was a minute trace of his sin, the man perform certain good deeds to atone for this trace of sin. Rabbi Breisch obviously felt that a complete acquittal would not satisfy the man under discussion.[18]

A direct quotation from the original Responsum documents the psychological sensitivity of the rabbi.

> Thus we conclude that our man does not need to have pangs of conscience because this will lead to sadness, which is an even greater sin, because it harms him and diverts him from the service of God which has to be done joyfully.[19]

A second case also involves a guilty conscience. A man threw a Torah scroll he owned into a river to prevent the Nazis from burning it. Now he has pangs of remorse and feels he might have saved the scroll by hiding it. A rabbi told him that atonement was not neccessary and tried to alleviate his conscience since he had acted in good faith.

Among the desperate counseling issues presented to the rabbis were the following:

> Is a man whose only child is destined to be sent to the ovens permitted to redeem him by bribery, knowing that this would result in the death of another child? Is suicide permissible in order to avoid torture and death in the ovens or gas chambers?

THE *MUSAR* MOVEMENT

Rabbi Israel Salanter (born in Vilna, Lithuania, in 1840; died in Koenigsberg, Germany, in 1883), founder of the *musar* movement, was concerned with using psychology and certain techniques of personal and group change to bring about a state of repentance and ethical perfection, rather than with using counseling to restore or maintain emotional health.[20] Salanter had an intuitive appreciation of emotional factors that we today would call psychodynamic. Salanter taught that the emotions, "the dim area," are more compelling than reason, the "bright area." The masters of *musar,* usually teachers in Talmudic academies, were not anti-intellectual. They had to meet the intellectual challenge of Talmudic studies, but they also chose to concentrate on transforming their own moral character. The teachers were not opposed to the model of *talmid chacham,* the disciple of the wise. They simply believed that one also had to train the emotions, develop self-mastery, and do acts of practical morality.

One of Salanter's first moves was to recommend the establishment of a *musar shtibl* ("a room for moral deliberation"). He called on businessmen to meet at least once a week and reflect on the ethics of their transactions. Later, women too were to participate in these fellowships for moral instruction. The greatest development of the *musar* movement took place in Talmudic academies, where a number of therapeutic and moral training programs were established. Students would meet at least one hour a day to review the ethical literature by reciting passages, to sing melodies, and to evoke a receptive mood. Their spiritual exercises suggest certain features of the disciplines recommended for Jesuits by Ignatius. The students formed small groups for spiritual therapy, confessing sins, offering mutual encouragement, and pledging to achieve ever higher standards of personal ethics. Sometimes the penitents would have spiritual supervisors, or *mashgichim,* who would meet weekly with the students and monitor their soul-searching. Stimulated by the fervor of their fellow students, and challenged by the confronting and exhorting words of the supervisors, the students often developed a self-flagellating moral scrupulosity.

Beyond the introspective searching, the *musarniks* (followers of *musar,* or ethics) were also expected to engage in public activities demonstrating how morally blameless they were trying to be. The *musar* movement developed into "an entire education system, based on, and aiming toward integration and subjection of the youthful emotions to a deeply instilled emotional defense system of a rigoristic Jewish life according to Halakah."[21] In some communities, the devotees of the movement engaged in practices we would associate with religious revivalists. They would proclaim their pietistic and moral enthusiasm by shouting in the streets, *"Gaaveh! Gaaveh!* [Pride! Pride!]. Don't act with pride! Cultivate the virtue of humility and cleanse your souls!"

The following statements attributed to Salanter convey the quality of introspection and self-confrontation that marked the *musar* movement.

> From your heart which follows its own beat, you can infer an understanding of the whole world and all its being.

> A person lives with himself for seventy years but cannot recognize himself.

> It is more difficult to change a single character trait than it is to study the entire Talmud.

> A mite of reason is drowned by a sea of will and desire.

> If you wish to excel over another, don't dig a pit for him; set a ladder up for yourself.

> If the study of ethics [*musar*] doesn't fully conquer sin, at least it takes away the joy of sinning.

> [After the Day of Atonement was over]: I feel as though a stone has been lifted from my heart.

> Before learning *musar,* I blamed the world, but not myself. After beginning to learn it, I blamed myself but judged the whole world on the side of merit.[22]

COUNSELING AND HASIDISM

Only in relatively recent Jewish history, in the period of the Hasidic movement in eastern Europe in the late eighteenth and nineteenth centuries, do we discern a pattern of counseling that at least approaches the person-centered counseling of today. The Hasidic rebbe was to be distinguished from other religious counselors because he was endowed with magic powers reflecting the imagery and ideology of a special faith system. He enjoyed charismatic power because of the person he was and the reputation he gained through his healing and because people ascribed to him certain intercessory powers.

In the interaction between the Hasidic master and the Hasid, we encounter a fully developed counseling relationship. There were some elements of this relationship in the *musar* movement, but by and large the supervisors, or *mashgichim,* were not charismatic personalities and the book or the text was still more important than the counselor. The following story is attributed to Rabbi Salanter:

> Both the Hasid as well as the Mitnagid [opponent of the mystics] are deserving of punishment. The Hasid because he asks "Why do I need the Book [The Torah] when I have the Rebbe?" The Mitnagid because he asks, "Why do I need the Rabbi when I have the Book?"

While Hasidism was not by definition anti-intellectual, it was distinguished by the special relationship that existed between the Hasid and the rebbe. The reader may be familiar with stories of Hasidic counseling translated and recast by Martin Buber. An extensive study of counseling in Hasidism was completed in 1968 by Rabbi Zalman Schachter, now of Temple University.[23]

We can find many features akin to psychotherapy in the personal encounter between the master and the Hasid. Unlike the sages of the Talmud, the rebbe was not concerned with encounters as vehicles for teaching. He was involved in a therapeutic system. The advice he gave was often grounded in biblical and rabbinic wisdom, but the goal was salvific. Cure came about from face-to-face contact between a charismatic personality and an individual Jew who felt free to come for personal help with any difficulty in living.

An elaborate ritual choreographed the approach of the Hasid to the Hasidic master. The Hasidic Jew believed that the master could rescue him from anxiety, help him in financial disaster, secure for him a place in the world to come, and heal any ailment of his body or soul. He believed in the charisma of the master as part of his assumptive system. Was this transference? If so, it was culturally reinforced by reputation, by faith, and by the mystique associated with the life and work of a particular master. Even today individual Hasidim will make pilgrimages to the courts of their favorite masters.

The counseling procedure included securing an appointment, writing down a description of one's problems on a piece of paper called a *quittel,* having the secretary bring the *quittel* into the private study of the master, and waiting for an invitation for the direct personal meeting (*yehidut*). The sequence of the *yehidut* included the reading of the *quittel,* a discussion of its meaning with the Hasid, the offering of counsel, or *etzah,* and a blessing at the time of the dismissal of the Hasid. The transaction often included the payment of a fee to the master. The faith placed in the master generated confidence that problems could be solved. The Hasid believed that special merit of the healer can provide the needed therapy.

Only part of their assumptive world was derived from classic Jewish texts. The Hasidic masters formulated their own diagnoses of the dynamics of depression, sickness, and human failure. A novice acquired counseling expertise by becoming an apprentice to a recognized master. In addition to religious teachings and symbols, the rebbes used psychological intuition and, on occasion, even magic. From all evidence, they exhibited an empathy for the needs of others which earned them intense loyalty.

The psychological insight of the masters is fascinating. Sensitive to their own dynamics, they were intuitively aware of what we would call problems in countertransference. One rebbe reported that he could almost always find an echo of a Hasid's problem in himself. The second Lubavitcher Rebbe made the following confession regarding his own emotional life:

> The basis by which I can listen to people's problems, sins, and worries is that I can always look into myself and find a disposition for the same problem within me. The last Hasid I listened to told me such a heinous story that I could not find any similarity to his life within me. And upon that realization, I was mortified, because this not only meant that such a similarity did exist, but that it lay deeply repressed within me.[24]

Self-knowledge and a capacity for profound empathy made it possible for the master to do counseling with a degree of sophistication that would do honor to a veteran analyst.

> The Rebbe himself does not take credit for the *etzah*. Like R'Pinhas of Koretz, he will say, quoting Bahia, "When a man conducts himself properly, he can see with a 'non-eye' and hear with a 'non-ear.'" Therefore, when a Hasid comes to ask an *etzah*, I hear how he himself tells me how to answer him. This is a function of the Rebbe's empathy with the Hasid. Like Carl Rogers, who believes that within the client resides the solution to his problem, R'Pinhas believes that the Hasid too brings with him his own solution. The Rebbe need only reflect to him the solution that exists in his own being.[25]

A special aspect of the interaction between the Rebbe and the Hasid is the *hitkashrut* (investment or preparation). It is a form of trial identification demanding great psychic exertion. Only when the master experiences the Hasid's problem deeply within himself can he intervene therapeutically.

> When the men of our covenant [euphemism for Hasidim] enter into *yehidut* and reveal the things that plague their hearts in their innermost being, each one according to his state, then each thing they tell me I must find in myself in its subtle form, or in the subtle form of the subtle form. It is impossible to answer him [the Hasid] and give him something to mend his ways and truly order his life until one mends this matter first in oneself, and only then can one give an *etzah* and a *tiqun* [prescriptive recommendation].[26]

The following anecdote anticipates the distinction modern-day psychotherapists make between intellectual insight and internalized, gut-level learning.

> A Habad Hasid once came to visit R'Mendl of Kotzk. In the course of their discussion the Rebbe, dealing with the Hasid's prayer life, asked him what the *Shema* meant to him. The Hasid replied with a lengthy discourse of book learning. Impatiently, R'Mendl interrupted him and said: "That's all very well. This is what it means to your head. But what does it mean to your *puppik* [umbilicus].[27]

Gestalt therapists frequently use the concept of "owning your own projections or your own desires." The following statement by the Berditchever Rebbe suggests the need for such "owning": "To a Hasid who complained that he suffered from impure, alien thoughts, he said: 'Alien? They are not alien—they are *yours*.' "[28]

In matters of confrontation, the Hasidic rebbe moved slowly. He appreciated how strong the compulsion to sin could be. The instinct of doing good—the *yetzer tov*—was feeble at best. The master might be persuaded that to confront a particular Hasid with his sins would accomplish nothing. Instead, he would build a solid therapeutic alliance. The ultimate goal was change in behavior, not labeling or berating the sinner. One of the Hasidic masters paid a visit to Rabbi Moshe Leib Sassover in order to learn when not to confront a sinner. Rabbi Sassover explained:

> What you say, I also saw; yet if I had told him (the sinner) this right away, he would not have been able to give up his sin, and he would no longer be able to come here. Thus, his way to *t'shuvah* [repentance] would have been blocked. But if I show him love, he may some day consider: "If the rebbe knew how sinful I am, he would not show me such love. I must become a better man so that I may deserve his love."[29]

The Kotzker Rebbe has left a legacy of brilliant counseling insights. Here is one about the power of God:

> One day a man complained to the Baal Shem about his son. He had discarded the path of piety. His conduct had become un-Jewish.
> "What shall I do, Rebbe?" he asked.

"Do you love your son?"

"Of course I do."

"Then love him even more."[30]

The Master of the Good Name—the leading personality of the Hasidic movement—demonstrated the most complete acceptance of his fellow man: "'Even the most impious of men is as dear to me as your only son is to you,' the Baal Shem Tov once said to a disciple."[31]

The Kotzker Rebbe never offered facile theological explanations. He refused to act as an intermediary between a person and a seemingly cruel God.

> Once a man came to Reb Mendl and poured out his heart. His wife had died in childbirth, leaving him with seven children and an infant. He himself was in rags.
>
> "I cannot console you over such cruelty," said the Rebbe. "Only the true Master of Mercy is able to do it. Address yourself to Him."[32]

What of more recent and contemporary rabbinical counseling? A complete account would include references to the Jewish Science Movement, to the contributions of the late Joshua Loth Liebman, author of *Peace of Mind,* to the synthesis of psychoanalysis and Judaism, to my own writings on empathy, to the efforts of Orthodox rabbis to compare and reconcile the codes of Judaism with the theory and practice of counseling, to the *havurah* (small-group) approach to counseling in the synagogue, as well as to the flow of articles and books by Reform rabbis dealing with all aspects of counseling and representing every variety of psychological theory.

In this age of psychology, people increasingly turn to rabbis for help in mastering difficulties in living. In such situations, the rabbinical role overlaps with the work of psychologists, social workers, and psychiatrists. Rabbis are now asking how deeply they wish to be involved in helping individuals and families work through personal problems. They face serious decisions when such help involves long-term counseling and leads to complications in transference. The problems facing rabbis on this issue differ little from those faced by Protestant or Catholic counselors.

In a single interview, religious counselors may find themselves dealing with many needs, some of which may be contradictory and difficult to identify: needs for catharsis, for rescue, for expert information, for healing, for relieving or firming up conscience, for support, for reinforcement, for judgment, for friendship. The list goes on. How rabbis meet these expectations is uncertain. Viewed from the perspective of Jewish tradition, they stand on the shoulders of spiritual giants.

CHAPTER 4

Show Me Thy Ways

Whence do we know that if a man sees something unseemly in his neighbor, he is obliged to reprove him? If he rebuked him and did not accept it, whence do we know that he must rebuke him again? The text states: "surely rebuke" all ways. (Arakin 16b)

R. Jose b. R. Hanina said: Reproof leads to love, as it says, Reprove a wise man, and he will love thee (Prov. IX, 8). Such indeed is R. Jose b. R. Hanina's view, for he said: *Love unaccompanied by reproof is not love.* (Genesis Rabbah [Vayera] 54:3)

Their first exposure to psychological theory has a way of immobilizing rabbis and ministers. Some are shocked when they feel a tension between principles and persons. Others, on looking into Freud's writings, suspect an inherent threat to moral principles and lose no time in making clear that their loyalty is to religion and not to the relativism and neutrality of the psychotherapist.

Caricatures abound. Therapists see pastoral counselors violating the patient's autonomy. Rabbis and pastors have been known to impute amorality and ethical nihilism to psychotherapists.

We see one possible resolution to the question of direction in counseling in these words from R. Jose b. R. Hanina: "Love unaccompanied by reproof is not love." But there are problems here too. What attitudes and what behaviors are we reproving? If our goal is to judge and we are reasonably sure of the principles we have in mind, how do we offer reproof most effectively to the people we would counsel? Was Rabbi Hanina a moral absolutist who believed that all a teacher must do is apply authoritative principles to specific situations? Or was he suggesting that loving others may lead us to avoid even the suggestion of moral judgment?

Don Browning suggests that the time has come to swing the pendulum back in the direction of a moral concern. He speaks of the importance of *moral inquiry* as contrasted with the "rigid application of unexamined rules."[1]

INTRODUCING VALUES

How much initiative rabbis should take in introducing questions of right or wrong in their counseling is an issue. We shall approach this question with suggestions drawn from Jewish sources as well as from leaders of the Christian pastoral counseling movement.

Two problems are involved. First, how shall we introduce religious values into our dialogue? And second, if values can be introduced—without doing violence to the counseling relationship—what specific values shall be presented? We are confronted with problems in technique as well as with problems of content. If you are completely committed to basic religious principles (a "principlist"), it is less important for you to consider what impact the discussion of principles has on your counselees. As a *principlist,* your principles are irrevocable, so the counselees' reactions are not going to lead you to reconsider your judgments. If you intend to indoctrinate counselees, you will use every persuasive technique available, including personal charisma. If the other person resists your approach, your ingenuity and your power to influence are challenged, and you become even more insistent.

If, on the other hand, you are a *consequentialist,* you may be equally convinced that the values you represent are valid, but you are prepared to discuss them, to explore with the counselee what their consequences would be, and to determine empathically how the counselee responds to them. Is it fair to say that the *consequentialist* is more interested in the person than in the principle? It hardly seems so. The *principlist* might as easily reply that a major principle of religion is love of one's neighbor. Is it a question of principles *versus* persons?

When Browning speaks of "resurrecting the ancient Hebrew images of the sage, of the scribe, and the Pharisee," he may be suggesting that these types of religious leaders were concerned only with moral inquiry. Rabbi Hanina's observation makes us appreciate that love was a powerful theme in the ethos and the theology of the rabbis. Judaism includes both love and moral inquiry. An issue we must still examine is the difference between moral inquiry and reproof (*tochacha*). The distinction may not be great because so much depends on the empathy of the pastoral counselor.

Rabbis tend to see themselves as *morae derech*, mentors of values and defenders of social justice. They are concerned with ideal behavior between person and person and among groups and communities. They feel called on to persuade, influence, and change people. They are symbols of the conscience. When they read from the Torah and the Prophets and when they preach, they exhort their congregations to make ethical choices and to conform to the mandates or guidelines of Judaism. They see themselves as change agents, using training in ethics *and* skill as communicators in order to evoke a religious and moral response to both personal and communal issues. Even if they are unsure of their position on specific issues, uncertain of the way they should apply or interpret Judaism—especially if they are not Orthodox rabbis and do not feel irrevocably bound by the disciplines of the *Halacha* (law)—they still feel concerned with moral issues and ethical dilemmas.

In Judaism, the issues of conscience and guilt in psychotherapy have been addressed by Martin Buber. Buber's comments are directed toward secular therapists rather than toward rabbis or pastoral counselors, but his words could apply to those rabbis who see themselves only as clarifiers and empathizers.

Buber speaks of an existential guilt that is not and should not be accessible to any of the psychological strategies. He refers to the "Melanie case," where a therapist was successful in helping his patient cope with pain and "adjust"; the cost to her was losing the capacity for genuine relationships. Melanie had caused the breaking of the engagement of a man to another woman. The relationship she coveted did not last long. Melanie was herself ultimately supplanted by another woman and, following this experience, became emotionally ill. After she was treated by an analyst, her guilt feelings were dissolved, but she never learned how to relate to other persons as anything but objects to be manipulated. Commenting on this form of guilt-relieving therapy, Buber wrote: "I call this successful cure the exchange of hearts. The artificial heart, functioning entirely satisfactorily, no longer feels pain; only one of flesh and blood can do that."[2]

Erich Fromm, like Buber, was not a rabbi but was informed about Jewish concepts. He offered one of the earliest critiques of so-called adjustment psychology in his Terry Lectures, entitled *Psychoanalysis and Religion*. Although he had much to say about the disguises and rationalization that entangle the conscience, Fromm, unlike the beleaguered psychoanalyst denigrated by Buber, indicated that the issue of conscience has a place in therapy. He criticized the "cookbook approach" dissolving guilt and neglecting ultimate concerns:

> One thing must be made clear. There are no prescriptions which can be found in a few books about right living or the way to happiness. Learning to listen to one's conscience and to react to it does not lead to any smug and lulling "peace of mind" or "peace of soul." It leads to peace with one's conscience—not a passive state of bliss and satisfaction but continuous sensitivity to our conscience and the readiness to respond to it.[3]

The following situation dramatizes the issue of moral inquiry or of confrontation. By "confrontation" we do not mean hectoring or moralizing. If we confront, do we have to give up empathy?

A member of our temple board who has a family of his own

confides in us that he has been having an affair with one of his secretaries. We cannot assume that this act of adultery calls for pronouncing an immediate judgment of guilt. There should be no monolithic, single-minded response. The visitor in our study knows as well as we do that the Seventh Commandment places him in the wrong. What is appropriate for the rabbi? To listen impassively? To indicate his appreciation for the discomfort being experienced by the adulterer? To be a confessor? To point out the possible injustice being done to the man's mistress as well as to his wife and children, to say nothing of himself? Is the rabbi to receive the information as though he were the man's analyst who might see this behavior as a form of acting out that is symptomatic of unconscious conflict and self-esteem problems? The rabbi might also ask whether he is being manipulated by a man who wishes to test the furthest limits of his behavior.

If the rabbi assumes that the man feels genuine guilt, he would have to determine how his dialogue could facilitate change. Most important, the rabbi would have to understand why the congregant came to see him in the first place. As judge? friend? therapist? God? There is no manual for handling such issues. A genuine counseling orientation will call for the rabbi to make an effort to understand and not to terminate the interview by dismissing the offender with a *halachic* (legal) ruling replete with references to the codes.

The rabbi does not have to take a relentlessly tolerant position in such a case. Even within the limits of an hour or hour-and-a-half interview, the rabbi can respond in several ways and can participate on more than one level. If he is inclined to use a confrontational style, he can still respond without necessarily expressing negative and rejecting feelings. Should he choose, he could be quite firm without stopping the flow of communication. He could even offer a judgment without being judgmental.

To suspend making a judgment does not mean that one backs down from a moral responsibility or dodges taking a position that might not be congenial to the counselee. If the rabbi wishes only to convey a judgment or to make a ruling like a *dayyan* (judge), the interview can be ended in a few minutes and the rabbi can feel that he acted responsibly as a representative of Judaism. But a concern for consequences and a sophistication about the ways people change should prepare the rabbi to be more than the *dayyan*. If he can succeed in establishing and extending the dialogue, he may have a chance to be a catalyst for successful change. I am not suggesting that suspending or withholding judgment means that the rabbi should conceal his own position or refuse to state what he feels to be the position of Judaism in this area of sexual ethics. The interview not only may continue but can also proceed more effectively if the rabbi makes his own position clear and then gets on with the work that needs to be done.

The rabbi and the congregant need to discuss what alternatives are open and to collaborate on a solution. What if the rabbi and the congregant cannot agree on the proper course? After one or more empathic interviews, the congregant would most likely decide to terminate. Should the rabbi dismiss the congregant if he persists in attacking the rabbi's position or demands the rabbi's approval of his behavior? Here the provocation would be sharp. It is conceivable that in some cases a punitive, judgmental attitude might be indicated. The consequences should be analyzed carefully. If the individual seems to need punishment by an authority figure or parental substitute, the rabbi should ask whether gratifying that need would serve the best interests of the person. Also, the rabbi would have to do some soul-searching to see whether he is handling his anxiety about his own sexual temptations by inflicting verbal punishment on others.

We have been discussing this case from the point of view of a rabbi, not a psychoanalyst who conducts therapy in relationships that extend for hundreds of hours over many months. The goal of the analyst is to create the best possible conditions for the functioning of the patient's ego. The rabbi works under the assumption that the problem-solving capacities of the individual allow intelligent and rational discussion in the context of a supportive relationship, discussion that can clarify issues and lead to decisions. Rabbis are becoming sophisticated in psychodynamics, appreciating the symbolism of their roles. But their model, unlike that of the therapist, is the *moreh derech*, the guide rather than the facilitator.

CHOOSING VALUES

Erich Fromm believed that the psychoanalytic process shares with religion the goal of awakening the patient's sense of wondering and questioning. He wrote, "Once this sense is awakened, the patient will find answers which are his own."[4] Now the differences between religion and psychotherapy emerge. Congregants who come for pastoral counseling are members of a religious community, sharing concerns and common values. They will find answers—which they can internalize and make their own—but they do so in what Browning calls "a moral context." They have resources available to them because they share basic religious commitments with other members of their group. They are heirs to a storehouse of ethical and spiritual values. While they have freedom to choose, especially if their theology is liberal, they act within a certain reference group.

Theoretically, they could, like Spinoza, reject that group and fashion a radically new theology, but only a rare visionary sets off on unexplored paths. Nearly all of us find fulfillment within communities where participation, when not regimented but freely chosen, offers the elements necessary for a life style of integrity. In the words of Erik Erikson,

> Although aware of the relativity of all the various life styles which have given meaning to human striving, the possessor of integrity is ready to defend the dignity of his own life style against all physical and economic threats. For he knows that an individual life is the accidental coincidence of but one life cycle with but one segment of

history; for him, all human integrity stands or falls with the one style of integrity in which he partakes. The style of integrity developed by his culture or civilization thus becomes the "patrimony of his soul," the seal of his moral paternity of himself.[5]

The patient will find answers on his own, according to Fromm, and ultimately outgrow his need for his therapist. The patient acts autonomously. He is not involved in the moral values of his therapist, nor does he participate in the community of professionals who constitute his therapist's reference group.

Though intensive psychotherapy is a *depth* psychology dealing with longstanding problems of a few individuals, pastoral counseling should not be considered superficial. It does not usually deal with buried, inaccessible conflicts, nor does it aim to reconstruct psychological defenses. It does deal with profound and critical matters in character and personal commitment. Religion deals with ultimate issues.

Perry London has commented on the limited focus of psychotherapy. He views the work of his colleagues as doing "repairs," using a repertory of treatment methods that amount to "tactical devices." London observes that most therapists are not equipped to deal with questions of ethics and ultimate values and are probably not eager to get involved in them. At the same time, he does not indulge the rabbis of today, who in his opinion are losing their credibility because they too avoid moral questions.

> I would like to believe of my rabbi that his concern is with the totality of my life and what I wish and fear to do with it. If I am willing, as a congregant, to encounter him in that connection, and he can respond with no other thoughtful intelligence than I can get from psychotherapists, he makes himself and his spiritual tradition counterfeit and, thereby, diminishes both himself and me.[6]

More important than the claims and counterclaims of psychiatry are the issues of *what* moral values to represent and *how* to present them in the counseling encounter. Martin Buber, who dismissed Freud as a "simplificator," did not claim to have the answer to the question of what man is and what man is called to be. But Buber was confident that he could at least "point" in the direction where the seeker might look:

> I have no teaching. I only point to something. I point to reality. I point to something in reality that had not or had too little been seen. I take him who listens to me by the hand and lead him to the window. I open the window and point to what is outside.[7]

Even if rabbis have anguished over moral issues and have distilled some theologically acceptable position adequate for contemporary needs, they must still speak, listen, and check to see if what they say is received as they intend it to be. Then they must encounter the individual's reactions, both intellectual and affective. They must hang in for the duration of the dialogue without making pronouncements. When they do speak they can "let it float," and then wait to see if their words, or the message of Judaism as mediated through their words, can be used by the counselee.

Rabbis and other intellectuals often invest great energy in dialectic (Talmudic *pilpul*) and presume they have done all that needs to be done when they have proved their point and, to their own satisfaction, overcome the objections or mental reservations of the other. When we counsel, we confront people philosophically, but we meet them on other levels as well. There is more here than the play of first-class minds. We are engaged in a relationship in which fears, anxieties, and hopes are implicated heavily. When we use the Talmud and Midrash as Browning would have all of us do, we find, along with a sensitive concern for justice and truth, a highly rationalistic approach—congenial to the Disciple of the Wise but not always appropriate in counseling. Remember Israel Salanter, the founder of the *musar* movement in the nineteenth century, who pleaded for attention to the character of the Talmudic student and the rabbi on the grounds that intellectual analysis alone cannot make Judaism a living reality.

Rabbis have many opportunities to treat moral values when they preach, teach the confirmation class, consult with the finance committee of their board regarding salary increases for staff, and work with committees on civil liberties, housing codes, sexual equality, and so on. There are times and places when rabbis may argue, admonish, cajole, and, if they are so minded, shout and condemn, but confronting a counselee calls for restraint and great sensitivity.

You may know (or think you know) what is right, but when you speak with an individual who is painfully confused and blocked, you have to draw on more than expertise as a debater and a theological virtuoso. Psychoanalyst Michael Balint spoke about the "apostolic function" of the doctor working with his patients:

> It was almost as if every doctor had revealed knowledge of what was right and what was wrong for patients to expect and to endure, and further, as if he had a sacred duty to convert to his faith all the ignorant and unbelieving among his patients.[8]

Should rabbis respond this way when they speak with every individual who stops in to share a concern about personal issues or family life? Is a personal conversation just another chance to preach a single-minded message? It is so easy to get caught up in either/or situations when what may be needed is what Maurice Levine, of the Department of Psychiatry at the University of Cincinnati Medical School, used to call "the third alternative." There is no reason why rabbis cannot suggest alternatives and, as appropriate, quote passages from the Ethics of the Fathers or homilies from the Midrash to illustrate and reinforce their points.

But how are you to know whether the particular situation is a teachable moment? If you go ahead and deliver your favorite sermonette, what do you do next? Dismiss the person you have been talking to? The great master, Hillel (first century B.C.E.), was challenged by a heathen: "Teach me the whole Torah while I stand on one foot." Hillel, as a gentle and patient teacher, answered, "What is hateful to you, do not do to your neighbor; that is the whole Torah, while the rest is commentary thereof. Go and learn it."[9] A more empathic Hillel might have asked his interrogator to take a more comfortable position so that they might discuss the man's response to Hillel's statement.

People perceive rabbis as superego figures—internalized parent images, in the jargon of psychoanalysis. But rabbis are also seen as the representatives of God, even through the eyes of cynics and skeptics. Ordinarily as clergy we do not believe that everything we preach represents the "still small voice" of conscience, but the role of prophetic critic is one we esteem and find attractive. We easily fall into the parental role, chiding our congregants like errant children and reminding them that we take responsibility for their behavior. But we really cannot be effective moral teachers if we relish our authority and take satisfaction in what has to be a position of moral superiority. We often misfire (the usage speaks for itself), and instead of evoking genuine guilt and real responsibility we reinforce guilt feelings.

Empathic counseling, with a clear focus on where the other person actually is and what he or she is experiencing, opens the possibility of discussing guilt as an objective fact. When and if we take the symbolic parental role, we need to be clear about the risks of authoritarianism. Good parenting in families can lead to moral growth, but in the preacher-congregant situation the parental role can have the reverse effect: Guilt feelings are evoked and angry defiance surfaces. The old power struggle is reexperienced, and when moral issues are not worked through, congregants leave disappointed and resentful, sometimes passive and helpless.

Psychology can serve as a commentary on religious texts when their value and human meaning may have eluded us because the old passages are so familiar that we can teach them without a fresh consciousness of their message. Take as one example a discussion of guilt by Isaac Meir of Ger, a nineteenth-century Polish Hasid:

Whosoever talks about and reflects upon an evil thing he has done is thinking about the vileness he has perpetrated, and with what one thinks, therein is one caught—with one's whole soul one is caught utterly in what one thinks, and so he is still caught in vileness. And he will surely not be able to turn, for his spirit will coarsen and his heart rot, and besides this, a sad mood may come upon him. What would you do? Stir filth this way or that, and it is still filth. To have sinned or not to have sinned—what does it profit us in heaven? In the time I am brooding on this, I could be stringing pearls for the joy of heaven. That is why it is written: "Depart from evil, and do good"— turn wholly from evil, do not brood in its wake, and do good. You have done wrong? Then balance it by doing right.[10]

Note that this homily deals with depression, "a sad mood." The Hasidic master recognized that even if a sin may have been committed, no good cause is served by hanging on to guilt and by wallowing in self-abasement. Meir calls such guilt "filthy." Ruminating about guilt does nothing to transform character; it stands in the way of repentance and making restitution. In this homily, confrontation is balanced with consolation. Would the homily strike home, or would it be necessary to extend the conversation so that the insight might be worked through and assimilated? In counseling (as contrasted with preaching), we would explore the need to hold on to the guilt and to try and understand what is served by refusing to change. There is a grand image here of "stringing pearls for the joy of heaven," but we would need to follow up with questions and reflections to see whether the individual actually experiences liberation. In counseling, the homily could prime the flow of communication; its reality for you and me could be tested and experienced.

When rabbis are open and not defensive, they personify the qualities necessary for growth and change. The counselor's attitude can be part of the message. It is true that, in preaching, the members of the congregation can identify with the embodiment of the message in the person of the preacher; in counseling, where a helping alliance is formed, the personhood of the rabbi can be an even more powerful catalyst for change.

If physicians can be faulted for having the *furor therapeuticus,* the overwhelming and ultimately self-defeating urge to help or to cure, pastoral counselors in their concern for values can exhibit a *furor pedagogicus.* Pastoral counselors are eager to do what they have been trained to do, which is to teach, actively to guide the perplexed toward a way of life that is authentic, ethical, and in the case of rabbis also "Jewish." An excess of zeal to counsel points to something unresolved in the counselor's mind and can be a clear sign that he or she is not empathically connected to others.

VALUES VERSUS POWER

Rabbis feel comfortable giving advice consistent with their theology. Their comfort often leads them to prescribe for the problems of others without inquiring into their perceptions and their feelings. They work effectively when teaching a class and knowing in advance what text they will deal with when delivering a prepared sermon. The message is clear, and during the discussion points can be clarified, important points reinforced.

How different is the counseling situation? Even if rabbis know something about the personal background of the individual, they do not know what questions they will be asked or what kind of dilemma or crisis their congregant is experiencing. They have no time to "get set." They realize they will be dealing not just with ideas and facts but also with inner experiences not easily appreciated. For leaders accustomed to speaking and directing, it is unsettling not to be able to anticipate or manage the flow of the conversation or even to know what is really expected of them.

As teachers and preachers, rabbis have a priori messages to deliver. They are trained to seize each occasion as an opportunity for teaching some truth or insight. They use psychology in preaching, but in counseling the agenda is different. Instead of prescribing for the needs of a community, rabbis now confront individuals or families who are evidently in discomfort or distress but whose actual needs are by no means clear, to themselves or to their counselors. For those in distress, there is no balm packaged for instant use. They may already know the rabbi from sermons and classes; when they come for counseling they expect attention to be given to them and to what they are experiencing now. Often they give up hope of satisfaction because the rabbi appears to know in advance what they are going to say and is ready with an incisive answer. Rabbis might take the advice given by Erich Fromm to students at the Hebrew Union College. "Surprise the members of your congregation," said Fromm. "Don't conform to their stereotypes. If you do, you'll inevitably disappoint them. Don't respond in a standardized, so-called 'rabbinical' style."

Should rabbis transform counseling sessions into opportunities for teaching? If rabbis have a genuine interest in helping, they may have to check a disposition to instruct at the wrong time and place. In the following dialogue, a young rabbi meets Pearl, a woman of eighty-two, who suffers from severe arthritis. The conversation takes place in a home for the aged, where Pearl lives. The rabbi is a chaplain at the home. Pearl is concerned about her forty-two-year-old bachelor son.

RABBI: Pearl, good to see you this afternoon. How are things?

PEARL: Hello, Rabbi Cohen. You're looking well today. How is your family?

RABBI: Fine, thank you. How have you been since I was here last week?

PEARL: Rabbi, I want to talk to you about my son. Did you know that he is a Kohen [of priestly descent]?

RABBI: No, I didn't.

PEARL: Well, he is, and you know a Kohen is not supposed to be near the dead. That's prohibited. But you know my son Bill went to a funeral of one of his friends, and he agreed to be a pallbearer.

RABBI: (trying to understand why the topic was being brought up): Yes . . .

PEARL: You know, Bill is feeling low. I think he is depressed. I think he realized later that as a Kohen he should not have agreed to be a pallbearer. He feels guilty. Rabbi, I am worried about him.

RABBI: I really don't think you should worry about this, Pearl. If your son is feeling low, it's probably something that we don't know anything about. I really think that his being a pallbearer had nothing to do with it. Moreover, you know that we Reform Jews do not follow many of the Orthodox practices, including the laws regarding the Kohen. I hope Bill feels better soon.

PEARL: He really shouldn't have done it as a Kohen. I think he forgot and then he remembered, and now he feels badly. I'm sorry he did it.

RABBI: Now, Pearl, really . . .

PEARL: Rabbi, I just think that this is the time when maybe we should do something. I'd like to make a contribution to some charity. I think it would help things.

RABBI: Pearl, you can make a contribution to charity if you wish, but I can tell you it's not necessary to do anything right now of that kind because you feel that there is a connection between Bill's serving as a pallbearer and his present mood. If you made a contribution for that reason, you would be showing that you are almost superstitious. Make a contribution if you like, but really, don't do it on the grounds that it would be good for your son, Bill, or that it would make up for any guilt on his part. That is just not in the spirit of liberal Judaism. I think you know that, Pearl.

The rabbi believed that Pearl was anxious because she held on to an outdated theology. To alleviate her feelings of guilt and discomfort, he offered her a theology that would spare her the consequences of holding an authoritarian belief system. Although Pearl was a liberal Jew, she retained some of the customs of more traditional Judaism. The rabbi did not see this meeting as a time for listening and for support. He felt it was a teaching moment.

The role of confronter, critic, or judge comes easily to rabbis and pastors. The role attracts them, in part, because it gives them what they assume is control over others. In this case, the rabbi took charge of Pearl's situation, admonishing her, directing her, and exercising control over her proposed actions.

The rabbi who was visiting Pearl might be given the benefit of the doubt. He may have sincerely and consciously intended to provide cognitive therapy. But we must ask whether he needed to use this face-to-face meeting as an occasion to pry Pearl loose from traditional religious practices. Was the rabbi's diagnosis correct? Was what Pearl needed at this moment a lesson in "liberal" theology? Did she really believe that contributing to a charity in the name of her son would in some way mitigate the punishment for violating a taboo? The act of charity might relieve Pearl of her anxiety over her son. It would relieve her frustrated maternal desire to help. Would the rabbi's image of himself as a fearless champion of religious truth have been diminished if he had listened and responded empathically?

Can we assume that clergy are always objective in making moral judgments? When we find ourselves repeatedly trying to control others, are we not rationalizing narcissistic needs? How do we show respect for the other person? The classical rabbis used to say that he who greets his fellow man should consider himself as greeting the *Shechinah* (Divine presence). In the Ethics of the Fathers, the Mishnaic masters advise us to greet everyone with a pleasant countenance.

WHAT PLACE FEELING?

No doubt some rabbis are temperamentally incapable of suspending their cognitive, analytic, and critical skills in order to empathize with persons in pain. They may choose to hammer away at people's defenses. The illustration I think of is the thoughtlessly aggressive philosophy instructor who ridicules freshman students when their logic is sloppy. The qualities that might dazzle a congregation with their flair, drama, and use of brilliant homilies are not the same qualities ordinarily useful in counseling.

Rabbis cannot be faulted for following the tradition of the wise disciples who esteemed intellectual skills highly. The same sages who were enemies of disorder in thought and behavior in Freud's metaphor were believers in the power of the ego to sit in the saddle and take full charge. To say that we need to appreciate the subjective emotional components in other people's behavior and feelings, as well as in our own, is not to downgrade the vast intellectual achievements of rabbis, philosophers, and scholars.

Why the bind of either/or thinking? Rabbinical counseling does not call for concessions to the nonrational or anti-intellectual, nor does it mean that tough-mindedness has to give way to soft sentimentality. Rigorous intellectuals have the same repertory of feelings and needs as the ordinary person who happens to be temporarily blocked in his or her problem-solving. Elie Wiesel recounts a story of the Hasidic master who empathized with a student outraged by the world's evil:

> To the desperate young student he had said: "I know there are questions that remain open; I know there is a suffering so scandalous that it cannot even have a name; I know that one can find injustice in God's creation—I know all that as well as you do. Yes, there are reasons enough for a man to explode with rage. Yes, I know why you are angry. And what do I say to you? Fine. Let us be angry. Together."[11]

In his *Guide to the Perplexed,* Maimonides appears as a philosopher who has confronted the basic issues of theodicy and concluded that much human distress comes from the error of attributing evil to God. He offers his philosophy as cognitive therapy, suggesting that he who holds rational concepts will be spared psychic pain. But let us put the *Guide to the Perplexed* aside and look at Maimonides the man in a letter written in 1170, eight years after the drowning of his brother David in the Indian Ocean. There we gain an appreciation of Maimonides as a flesh-and-blood, feeling and experiencing individual. Suddenly he appears less formidable, less cerebral, more accessible. We now can recognize him as one of us, vulnerable and sensitive to hurt.

> On the day I received that terrible news I fell ill and remained in bed for about a year, suffering from a sore boil, fever, and depression, and was almost given up. About eight years have since passed, but I am still mourning and unable to accept consolation. And how should I console myself? He grew up on my knees, he was my brother, he was my student. . . . Now, all joy has gone. He has passed away and left me disturbed in my mind in a foreign country. Whenever I see his handwriting or one of his letters, my heart turns upside down and my grief awakens again. In short, "I shall go down to the nether world to my son in mourning" (Gen. 37:35).[12]

Without this letter we would only be able to know Maimonides the philosopher, the consummate master of dispassionate ratiocination who appeared to live by a liberating theology. What might Maimonides have needed in order to work through and complete his private grieving? He was his own cognitive therapist endowed with elegant analytic powers. Nevertheless, he still wanted an empathetic response because in another letter he angrily chided a friend for not sending him a letter of consolation.

STRAIGHTENING OTHERS OUT

We have been discussing two kinds of confrontational counseling: one moral, the other logical. Another option is to make it possible for people to express their pain and frustration. We can empathize and restrain ourselves from actively instructing and guiding others. If we do not, we underestimate the value of catharsis or ventilation face-to-face with someone we trust and who we feel cares about us. Must we always straighten people out? Do we really believe that people come to us in childlike dependence, expecting us to bail them out theologically, emotionally, or philosophically? We tend to cut complaining short, in part because we have been trained to intervene. Even counselors with years of experience feel underemployed when they are listeners. When we move in and actively deal with the childlike behavior of our congregants, we feel fulfilled in our parental role; we make things right for the child who is hurting.

In our more reflective moments we know that our presence offers reassurance and that our own stability models an alternative response to helplessness. Most of us have enough psychological knowledge to appreciate the fact that when we rush to ease the pain felt by others we may be attempting to cope with our own anxieties which are triggered by getting even slightly close to the pain of our friends. We can reach the limits of our own tolerance for intense emotion, and although we want to appear confident, secure, and strong, we often know that inside we are restless and much prefer calmer and more manageable scenes. James Dittes says that it is more difficult for clergy than for anyone else to let groans be groans.

> To enter into them as they are, to let their rhythms and energies find their own course, to minister *through* the groans not *to* them. . . . Clergy have difficulty finding meaning and call arising out of the experience of others—*"God's own people"*—because they are accustomed to the expectations of professors, church members, and their own inner yearnings, to locating initiative and responsibility for ministry in themselves.[13]

Listening to another person's groans is not the same as giving in to what might appear to be their helplessness. To participate in their experiences does not necessarily mean that we get stuck in the same deep pit of misery. The empathizer is not damaged by identifying with others, vicariously sharing their pain. Refusing to empathize may mean that we are trying to rescue ourselves from some perceived or imagined trouble. It may also mean that we hide behind the role of consoler, giving ourselves comfortable distance from the heat and intensity of the pain others bring to us. We are trained to be teachers of the ignorant, to be guides for the intellectually confused, to be confronters of those who are "at ease in Zion." Can we also reach out to those who need us as companions in the search for meaning, for self-esteem, and for moral integrity?

We are on tap, so to speak, for personal consultation. People seek us out as emergency resources in times of crisis and transition. The counseling we do is intermittent, growing out of special situations. We have an enduring, open-ended relationship with our congregants and touch their lives at many important intersections. Counseling is only one expression of our unitary master-role. We can be similar at times to therapists, but there is no role in modern society as pervasive and comprehensive as ours. Some find their way out by becoming specialists in pastoral counseling; most of us stick by a unitary role, as broad and as deep as religion itself.

CHAPTER 5

Empathy: Where Religion and Psychotherapy Converge

It is said that on a particular *erev* Yom Kippur the great Hasidic master, Levi Yitzhak of Berditchev, stood outside his door early in the afternoon preparing himself spiritually for the Yom Kippur service. A tailor passed along the street looking for some business. "Have you anything to mend?" "Anything to mend?" Levi Yitzhak began to cry. A disciple who was standing nearby was puzzled. "My master, why are you crying?" "My soul needs mending and there is no one who can do it for me." (Samuel H. Dresner, 1974, p. 180, as retold by Daniel J. Silver)

One day a neighbor who is a psychoanalyst met me on the street and greeted me warmly. Then, smiling and appearing quite pleased with himself, he asked me, "Well, Rabbi, any breakthroughs in religion lately?" I did not know what, if anything, he wanted me to say. I believe that I smiled, perhaps tolerantly, accepting the doctor's teasing but also acknowledging to myself how enthusiastic he must have been about the achievements of Freud and his successors. Freud looked on himself as a liberator and said that discoveries such as his come about only once in a lifetime. But Heinz Kohut, founder of the self-psychology group in the psychoanalytic movement, had a different perspective. Shortly before his death in 1981, he wrote: "Psychoanalysis has hardly yet scratched the surface of the fascinating mystery of man."[1] If Judaism does not have breakthroughs, it does have a rich tradition that continues to explore that mystery.

The Haggadists of the Midrash, the Halachists of rabbinic

literature, the philosophers, poets, ethical writers, and the Hasidic masters have all added to that legacy. The major themes of Judaism—among which are love, empathy, anti-idolatry, and respect for the creative intelligence—continue to be taught and continue to inform the Jewish experience. Nothing has happened to make them obsolete. They address us now.

The task of *tikkun hanefesh,* perfection of the soul, is unremitting. As people turn their attention to the life of the interior—the personal, the emotional—they ask increasingly for counsel if not for therapy. Because of this emerging need, empathy on the part of the rabbis toward their congregants takes on a fresh if not urgent significance. Jewish teachings on love, empathy, and ethics are rich lodes that rabbis can mine to enhance their preaching and their teaching. Such themes can also influence their counseling, but literacy in the sources does not guarantee that the rabbinical counselor will be effective. A well-stocked, disciplined intelligence is a superb asset, but more than information and reasoning skill are needed.

Fortunately the clinical experience of therapists and analysts over the past several decades has brought to light some realities about the process of human communication, long ago appreciated by poets and artists but now tested, documented, and systematically conceptualized by scientists. Insight from the disciplines of social science and psychotherapy can make rabbis, always committed intellectually to empathy, more likely to be able to translate what they believe into day-by-day interaction with people. Researchers in psychology have made no real breakthrough respecting the phenomenon of empathy, but they have provided techniques for identifying and then monitoring the empathic process in dialogue.

Rabbis and ministers would do well to inform themselves in a more organized way of the nature of empathy and to apply this new conceptualization to their religious work. Contemporary psychology provides a new commentary on old religious texts and offers a new "spiritual" discipline to qualify the rabbi to do "practical theology" better.

This is not a call for the clergy to rush to imitate the analyst, to surrender their own identity, or to neglect prayer, meditation, study of the Torah, or the practice of *mitzvoth* (commandments). We do not need medical or clinical psychologists to legitimate the priorities we have chosen. We take responsibility for our own ministry, but also understand that by adapting psychological principles to our own role we can enhance the effectiveness of our work. Religion *should* be open to new modes and new insights from which it can choose judiciously.

As counselors we are indebted to psychoanalysis for various methods of studying individual lives over long periods. Among the new techniques is empathic identification, a mode of understanding which uses subjective experience in a highly disciplined process. Another is the steady and honest probing of transference and countertransference reactions. No one in the helping professions can afford to neglect the discipline of self-study and the constant scrutiny of response and motivation. Most liberal clergy already speak the patois of psychology. What remains is to gain experience in self-study and a fuller awareness of the many subtleties of interaction that can escape us, as they also escape professional therapists who become careless through routine.

Beginning with Freud and continuing in the form of published reports of extended psychotherapy, case studies are a valuable resource that we in religion are only now beginning to appreciate. Psychological research has also extended and deepened our understanding of the human personality, in particular the stages in the evolution of the growing, maturing self. Structural theories of personality have been formulated. The ferment among competing ideologies in psychoanalysis and psychology, the recent questioning of the medical model, and the exploration of new paradigms for family therapy increase the potential for a richer grasp of the nature of human relations.

How much psychological sophistication should be employed by rabbis who counsel? Rabbis who contemplate major counseling commitments should consider personal analysis in order to identify their blind spots and become alert to transferences. Extended supervision under a competent therapist would be a sine qua non. Intensive training in psychotherapy, on the other hand, has been known to lead to overidentification with the secular therapist, touching off role conflict. Worse, such training can generate ambivalence toward the mystic and symbolic components in religion.

Even those rabbis who wish to do no more than the counseling that is an everyday part of their work might still consider psychotherapy. I have known rabbis, baffled and frustrated in their work, whose careers have been turned around because of successful therapy. They have developed greater inner resources and have become less dependent on the approval of others, less vulnerable to criticism and hostility, and less perfectionistic in their demands on themselves. Status and authority cease to be vexing issues for them. Thus they free up their energies and enhance their potential for empathy.

If therapy is not always indicated, then at least some form of supervision, consultation, and collaboration with other professionals is probably desirable for *all* clergy. As Alastair Campbell writes so perceptively,

> To help us in this discipline we need a trusted friend who will not let us hide, or a small group in which anything can be freely said. In our private reflection, we need to learn to pray in a way that is intimate, rough-and-ready, perhaps a little impertinent (if we suppose that God favors politeness!). . . .[2]

Is a little psychology a dangerous thing? Would clinical supervision and personal confrontation inhibit rabbis, making them self-conscious to a fault? There is a romantic view which suggests that the clergy are free-spirited artists whose spontaneity can only be stifled if their work is subjected to objective analysis. In religion, we sometimes see ourselves as heirs to the prophets, called to God's service and destined to speak as the spirit moves us. But can we play our spiritual flutes without the practice that even a Rampal needs in order to produce his delicately soaring notes?

Some rabbis insist on referring to their vocation as "a calling" and reject the term "professional." Do they then counsel by the seat of their pants? They insist on the privilege of doing spiritual counseling and resist supervision as if it would put their religious authority at risk.

We who feel commissioned to call attention to moral values can often do with a bit of confrontation ourselves. Our ordination may give us symbolic authority, but it does not confer character on us. Speaking about Protestant counselors, Campbell says:

> Learning to care through fuller knowledge of self entails a discipline which comes naturally to us. It requires a degree of honesty about ourselves and about others which most conventional social encounters avoid. The Christian churches, despite their emphasis on confession and on loving others, tend to encourage insincerity, the hiding of true motives under a veneer of politeness and social respectability.[3]

Campbell adds that one of the greatest hazards in Christian pastoral counseling is verbosity: "We use words to distance ourselves from experience—our own and other people's—and so to lose the simple sense of nearness—nearness of nature, of other people, and of God."[4]

In the Jewish experience, Campbell's reference to "verbal games" is suggestive of *pilpul*, which in its negative sense means superficially clever, petty, and competitive argumentation. When rabbis are driven to share their enthusiasm for the Torah, they can impair dialogue by force-feeding their congregants. Out of excitement and zeal for Judaism, they can sometimes overwhelm their counselees with heavy doses of Jewish learning. Congregants may be impressed by the credentials of their rabbis but be unable to connect rabbinical teaching to the conflicts and stresses in their lives. Some rabbis are quick to use every personal encounter as one more opportunity for teaching Torah, but if they intend to counsel, they might become more aware of their lapses in empathy and take steps to reestablish the give and take of dialogue. Rabbis teach Torah when they deliver eulogies or explain the mourning customs of Jews, but when they make a bereavement call, need they unfailingly quote from Job? The heavy hand of didacticism can prevent the rabbi from making personal contact with the mourner. The master-disciple relationship is too much with us. A distinguished Orthodox rabbi, David Hartman, reported that in his rabbinic training he was carefully trained to answer Halakhic (Jewish law) questions. However,

> Upon entering the rabbinate, I was anxious to answer the great halakhic questions of the Jewish community. I waited with anticipation, but, to my dismay, no one came. I had answers; the problem was, I wasn't asked any questions. Finally I realized that the role of the rabbi was not so much to provide answers as to create questions.[5]

Rabbi Hartman, now professor of philosophy at the Hebrew University in Jerusalem, offers an empathic insight when he comments, "The task of the teacher is to listen before speaking. I had to forget my answers in order to hear the new questions."

In the Mishnah—Avoth, Ethics of the Fathers—we have a model of the ideal student of the Torah, whose attributes include "loving God, loving his fellow creatures, loving righteous ways, welcoming reproofs of himself, loving uprightness, keeping himself far from honors and [not letting] his heart become swelled on account of his learning."[6] The historic Jewish emphasis on elegant rationality can hamper the empathy of rabbis who counsel. At times, Judaism has given preeminence to the life of the mind, favoring dialectics to the neglect of the personal dimension and the affective component in human relations. The intellect is revered; personality is downplayed. Some balancing of mind and heart is necessary when rabbis add counseling to the range of their rabbinic responsibilities.

As scions of a great tradition of learning, rabbis take pride in carrying on the work of the sages. If they have more than the usual commitment to study and pursue their scholarship seriously, they may even add to the sea of Jewish learning. But if they intend to counsel, as many do, they need to have more than well-stocked minds.

When we enter into counseling relationships, we use more than our learning and our dialectical skills. We draw on our powers of feeling and of imaginative sympathy. So that we can assess situations objectively, we require the talent of identifying with others, of entering into the world of their experience, without losing our capacity for detaching ourselves from our emotional involvement. When we counsel, we must use "ourselves" as caring and compassionate persons. In order to use ourselves, we must be more than "studying machines," to recall Solomon Schechter's apt phrase.

Rabbis and ministers still enjoy symbolic authority. They are taken to be specialists in morality and theology. In counseling, the authority of their learning can lead them to overemphasize their role as moralists. They have much wisdom to dispense—the insights of religion, the visions of poets, the philosophic experience of great minds—but all this learning, even if shared with sincerity and with passion, is often less than the congregant wants to hear. In our sermons and our discussions, our counselees have already heard about religious answers and philosophic formulations. Then why do they come for counseling? Because even if they have the information they might need, they may not be able to use it. They are in conflict; they feel that they cannot think clearly. They want catharsis and relief from the anxiety they are experiencing; they want support, acknowledgment, and an empathic response from someone who cares and who may possibly even understand.

We rabbis do not possess ready-made answers to the problems of our people. We do not offer them prerecorded cassettes of advice ready for instant play. We need to encounter persons, not patients, to relate to them and to their inner worlds as guides. Our "counsel" should rarely be information or advice alone, even if at fifty we might be fit to give it, as the Mishnah reminds us. If we

spend most of our working hours teaching and preaching, we
have learned how to select in advance certain themes to be dis-
cussed. We are the stage managers. But in a counseling session the
time belongs to the counselee or the counselee's family; we do not
predetermine the agenda. We invite them to step in, but what
they come for is not a sermon, even if that is what they may leave
with.

In our own study of the Torah, we are advised not only to get
teachers but also to acquire companions. If our study is often best
done when another's mind shares our search for understanding,
how much more does counseling require the sympathetic participation of another mind and another heart. The rabbis were led to
make this interpretation of the Mishnaic prescription "Get yourself a companion."

> What does this mean? It teaches that a man should get a companion
> for himself; one who will eat with him, drink with him, read the
> Scriptures with him, study with him, lodge with him, and reveal to
> him all secret lore [literally, all of his secrets], the mysteries of the
> Torah and the problems of everyday life . . . whence do we know
> that when his companion corrects him and continues to read with
> him they both receive a good reward for their labor? Because it is
> stated, "Two are better than one; because they have a good reward
> for their labor."[7]

This passage primarily addresses the problem of the most effective way of studying the Torah, but it also conveys an appreciation
of the human need to confide in a trusting companion. I take this
as an awareness on the part of the sages of what can happen in
good counseling.

In counseling, rabbis should offer their learning and experience as part of the give and take of a personal encounter with
others. The relationship need not be that of master and disciple.
We can be companions in the search, fellow explorers, even
veteran travelers who walk alongside the seeker. Rabbi Leo Baeck
once said that the greatest gift of the rabbi is himself. We should

make no claims for authority. Although we cannot pretend to be equals, since it is the counselee who has come to us for help, nevertheless we can participate in a dialogue with total respect for the other. In the process our own horizons may be stretched. A Talmudic sage commented, "Much Torah have I learned from my Masters, more from my fellow students and from my disciples most of all!"[8]

Alastair Campbell has recently addressed himself to "the rediscovery of pastoral care." His recommendation concerning a different understanding of the character of the teacher's authority is one that we rabbis might take to heart:

> We have gone through a period of nervousness about any kind of directiveness, any notion that the individual needs to learn through an encounter with that which is other than self. We cannot return to simplistic contrasts between the knowledgeable and the ignorant, the wise and the foolish. But equally we must question the naive idea that we learn nothing from others, other than that which we already implicitly know ourselves. Instead of either of these extremes, I shall be suggesting that teachers must be companions on the same journey that we ourselves are making, and that their authority derives from their ability to be fellow travelers, friends and comrades on this journey.[9]

Until recently rabbis have failed to confront the challenge of dynamic psychology. In our counseling, we have taken our cue from the helping professions, adopting their methods and at times assuming their identities. Even when people call us "Rabbi," we have often listened to them as if we saw ourselves as therapists. One layman recently said, "Why are you shrinking me, Rabbi?" We often deprive our people of patient and searching *dialogue* about religious values in critical life situations.

Should rabbis wish to become therapists as well as religious counselors, they would have to take no less training than psychiatrists, psychologists, or psychiatric social workers. What might the goals of religious or rabbinical counselors be? To treat psychological illness? To treat patients as members of a team of experts? To be a referral agent? Is it their role to be available when therapists have done all they can, which at its best is to free up the ego of the patient to be able to function under the optimum conditions? "Freeing up the ego" of neurotically blocked persons requires a skill attainable only after specialized training. Nearly all rabbis who do counseling as a part of a master rabbinical role work with people who are not so severely restricted. In such cases we can feel justified in introducing Jewish values and perspectives. Should clinical supervisors point out to us that such intervention would not be appropriate in therapy, we could reply that we are not therapists. Once alerted to the risks of intervention, we can suggest values and alternatives as competent practical theologians.

Our people take us to be exponents of the Torah, even when we modify and supplement the tradition. We can invite our people, when they are thinking about critical issues in their personal lives, at least to look at the texts and ponder them. If Freud felt that some direction would be acceptable in the large-scale application of psychoanalytic therapy, should we rabbis hold back and even outdo the master in avoiding intervention? "It is very probable, too, that the large-scale application of our therapy will compel us to alloy the pure gold of analysis freely with the copper of suggestion."[10]

People will find us more helpful if they sense our empathy for them. Carl Jung once said that as a boy he despaired of talking with his father because his father always acted as if he knew in advance what was on his son's mind. Even if by chance we are familiar with data or information that is being told to us, we would do well to listen before speaking. People have a need to tell it to us. The flow of feeling would be interrupted if we showed impatience, flaunting our knowledge. The net effect would be a put-down.

A seasoned rabbinical counselor recently called my attention to a verse (1 Kings 19:12) which has something to say about human as well as divine communication.[11] The prophet Elijah had hidden in a cave on the mountainside. He had entreated God to appreciate his dedication and to grant him protection. God called to him and asked him to stand before him on the mountain. But where was God? He was not in the strong wind; he was not in the earthquake. The Lord was not in the fire; "and after the fire a still, small voice."

Now in the Hebrew the last three words—"still, small voice"— can literally be translated as "the sound of thin (light, delicate) silence." Commenting on the meaning of this phrase, Rashi (1040–1105) ventured a guess as to what the text meant by the words "thin, small voice." According to the medieval commentator, those words were intended to tell us that Elijah "had heard the voice coming out of the silence."

Can we, rabbis and pastors, who would enter into the most caring, respectful, and direct communication, do less than allow our attentive silences to be heard?

Notes

INTRODUCTION

1. Quoted in Abraham J. Heschel, *A Passion for Truth* (New York: Farrar, Straus & Giroux, 1973), 276.

2. Leo Baeck, *The Essence of Judaism,* trans. Irving Howe (New York: Schocken Books, 1948), 211–12.

3. Joshua Loth Liebman, *Peace of Mind* (New York: Simon & Schuster, 1946), xi.

4. Ibid.

5. Shabbat 31a (italics mine).

6. Quoted in Nahum N. Glatzer, *Franz Rosenzweig: His Life and Thought* (New York: Schocken Books, 1953), 4 (Rosenzweig as translated by Glatzer); see also 225.

7. Sigmund Freud and Oskar Pfister, *Psychoanalysis and Faith* (New York: Basic Books, 1963), 61.

8. Ta'anith 22a. I have followed the translation of Jakob J. Petuchowski, *Our Masters Taught* (New York: Crossroad, 1982), 112.

9. Sifre, Ekeb, par. 49. I refer the reader to a now-classic article by the Hebrew poet Hayyim Nahman Bialik on the differences between the Halakah and the Haggadah, inadequately translated as "Law and Lore." Bialik's article, published originally in Hebrew in 1917, was translated into English and appeared in the *Contemporary Jewish Record,* vol. 7, no. 6 (December 1944). According to the poet, the Haggadah "counsels and reckons with human capacities and insights; its yes and no are flexible" (p. 663). He adds that "A Judaism that is only Aggadic is like steel heated in fire but never chilled. The heart's aspiring, good will, an elevated mind, inward love—all these are fine and significant things, if only they issue in *deeds,* deeds as hard as iron and in stern duty" (p. 679).

10. Menahoth 29b.

CHAPTER 1

1. David Weiss Halivni, "The Study of the Talmud and Jewish Mysticism" (Report of the Conference on the Jewish Tradition and Experience, Center for the Study of Democratic Institutions, Santa Barbara, Calif., September 10–12, 1973, mimeographed, unpaginated). Halivni continues: "He circumvents them. He acts them out through the study of the Torah which, true to the ambivalent nature of man, constantly vacillates between submission and assertion, between extolling the text to divine heights, and changing it through interpretation. This indirect way of tackling basic human problems, projecting them into, and subsuming them by the study of the Torah, may not be more effective than the mystic's way but it seems to us to be more elegant . . . and above all it places our everyday mundane activities theologically on a firmer ground."

2. Max Kadushin, *The Rabbinic Mind*, 3d ed. (New York: Bloch Publishing, 1972), 17ff.

3. For this and other rabbinic references concerning empathy, see Robert L. Katz, "Empathy in Modern Psychotherapy and in the Aggada," *Hebrew Union College Annual* 30 (1959): 191–215.

4. Sheldon H. Blank, "Doest Thou Well to Be Angry? A Study in Self-Pity," *Hebrew Union College Annual* 26 (1955): 38.

5. J. Abelson, *The Immanence of God in Rabbinical Literature* (London: Macmillan & Co., 1912), 283.

6. Moritz Lazarus, *The Ethics of Judaism*, trans. H. Szold (Philadelphia: Jewish Publication Society of America, 1901), pt. 2, p. 103.

7. Haggigah 5b.

8. Pesikta de Rab Kahana 116a.

9. Shabbat 31a.

10. *Gates of Repentance: The New Union Prayerbook for the Days of Awe* (New York: Central Conference of American Rabbis, 1978), 522.

11. Ibid., 108.

12. Avoth 3:1.

13. Erubin 13b. See also Avoth 4:22: "For without thy will wast thou fashioned, without thy will wast thou born, without thy will livest thou, without thy will wilt thou die, and without thy will art thou of a certainty to give an account and reckoning before the King of Kings, blessed be he."

14. Baba Metzia 59b, as translated by Petuchowski, *Our Masters Taught*, 43–44. (Italics mine.)

15. I am again indebted to Petuchowski. See Jakob J. Petuchowski, "Theology and Poetry in the Liturgy of the Synagogue," in Asher Finkel and Lawrence Frizzell, *Standing Before God* (New York: Ktav Publishing, 1981), 227–28.

16. Louis I. Newman, *The Hasidic Anthology* (New York: Charles Scribner's Sons, 1938), 57.

17. Moses Maimonides, *Mishnah Torah*, Laws Concerning Repentance, 7:4. The special virtue accorded the penitent calls to mind the New Testament parable of the prodigal son (Luke 15:11–32).

18. Yoma 86b.

19. Joseph Soloveitchik, *Al Hateshuvoh*, ed. P. Pelli (Jerusalem: World Zionist Organization, 1976), 183–85.

20. Sukkah 52a–52b.

21. Ibid., 51b–52a.

22. Arnold Jacob Wolf, "Psychoanalysis and the Temperaments of Man," in *Rediscovering Judaism: Reflections on a New Theology*, ed. Arnold Jacob Wolf (Chicago: Quadrangle Books, 1965), 147. Viewed psychologically, the rabbinic description of the evil instinct *(yetzer hara)* presents a case of projection. In commenting on Psalm 9, the Midrash Tehillim suggests that "no man sins unless a spirit of folly (madness) *enters into him.*" We sin only when we have been taken over by irrational forces. Both the "good" instinct and the "bad" instinct are seen as "attaching themselves" to us. The "bad" instinct enters us in infancy, while the "good" instinct enters us thirteen years later. The term "instinct" is misleading—both the "bad" and the "good" instincts are acquired.

23. Sotah 14a.

24. Shabbat 133b.

25. Jakob J. Petuchowski. See Report of the Conference on the Jewish Tradition and Experience, unpaginated.

26. Petuchowski, *Our Masters Taught*, 77–78.

27. Sanhedrin 26b.

28. Mechilta, ed. J. J. Lauterbach (Philadelphia: Jewish Publication Society of America, 1933–49), 2:178.

CHAPTER 2

1. Seward Hiltner wrote to me from Princeton on June 18, 1979: ". . . is there some kind of phrase you can find or coin that would do at least partial justice to the focus of your concern as a Jewish rabbi involved with

working with people in terms of healing or reconciling or even a bit of guiding? As you know, my search for an appropriate umbrella phrase went back to the older term pastoral theology. But the pastoral clearly is not in the Jewish tradition, and you Jews even use theology somewhat differently from the way we do." Hiltner went on to comment that ". . . any Jewish seminary that wants to do anything along these lines has to coin some fancy euphemisms of its own, not infrequently trespassing on medical terms in the process."

2. Sukkah 49b. *"Gemiluth hasadim* can be done with one's person and one's money." It is, therefore, both for the rich and the poor.

3. George H. Mead, *Mind, Self, and Society,* ed. Charles W. Morris (Chicago: University of Chicago Press, 1934), 296–97.

4. Mishnah Peah I, and Baraitot. These passages are included in the morning service of the traditional prayerbook.

5. Martin Buber, *Hasidism and Modern Man,* ed. and trans. Maurice Friedman (New York: Horizon Press, 1958), 248–49.

6. Leo Baeck, *The Essence of Judaism,* trans. Irving Howe (New York: Schocken Books, 1948), 211–12.

7. Samuel H. Dresner, *The Zaddik* (New York: Abelard-Schuman, 1960), 180.

8. Ibid., 177ff.

9. John Friedman, *The Good Society* (Cambridge: M. I. T. Press, 1979), 15.

10. Elie Wiesel, *Souls on Fire: Portraits and Legends of Hasidic Masters,* trans. Marion Wiesel (New York: Random House, 1972), 170–71.

11. As quoted in Walter Jackson Bates, *From Classic to Romantic* (Cambridge: Harvard University Press, 1956), 134–35.

12. Ketubot 105b. This is a wordplay. The actual text concludes with the word "bribe." The rest is an explanatory footnote.

13. Martin Buber, *Between Man and Man,* trans. Ronald Gregor Smith (New York: Macmillan Co., 1965), 17.

14. Ibid., 12–13.

15. Martin Buber, *The Knowledge of Man,* trans. Maurice Friedman (New York: Harper & Row, 1965), 183.

16. Gershom Scholem, "Three Types of Jewish Piety," *Ariel* (Jerusalem) 32 (1973): 5–24. Originally published in *Eranos Yearbook, 1969–72,* pp. 331–48.

17. Ibid., 9.

18. Ibid., 19.

CHAPTER 3

1. Leviticus Rabbah 34.

2. Nedarim 39a.

3. Midrash Shir Ha-Shirim 2:35. Compare this version with the text of Berakoth 5b: "R. Johanan once fell ill and R. Hanina went in to visit him. He said to him: 'Are your sufferings welcome to you?' He replied: 'Neither they nor their reward.' He said to him: 'Give me your hand.' He gave him his hand and he raised him. Why could not R. Johanan raise himself? They replied: 'The prisoner cannot free himself from jail.' [The rabbis observe that the patient cannot cure himself.]"

4. Moed Katan 27b.

5. Shabbat 151b.

6. Moed Katan 21b.

7. Sanhedrin 75a.

8. Leviticus Rabbah 9, as paraphrased by Petuchowski in *Our Masters Taught*, 93–94.

9. Shabbat 82a, as rendered by Petuchowski in *Our Masters Taught*, p. 12.

10. Jacob J. Neusner, *A History of the Jews in Babylonia*, vol. 2, *The Early Sassanian Period* (Leiden: E. J. Brill, 1966), 131.

11. Baba Bathra 12a.

12. Neusner, *History*, 2:77.

13. Sanhedrin 98a, as rendered by Petuchowski in *Our Masters Taught*, 110.

14. Louis Jacobs, *Theology in the Responsa* (London: Routledge & Kegan Paul, 1975), ix.

15. Ibid.

16. Ibid., 104.

17. Ibid., 187.

18. Alexander Guttmann, "Humane Insights of the Rabbis Particularly with Respect to the Holocaust," *Hebrew Union College Annual* 46 (1975): 437–38.

19. Ibid.

20. Arnold Rachlis, "The Musar Movement and Psychotherapy," *Judaism* 23 (1974): 337–45; Hillel Goldberg, "Toward an Understanding of Rabbi Israel Salanter," *Tradition* 16 (Summer 1976): 83–119; Mel Gottlieb, "Israel Salanter and Therapeutic Values," *Tradition* 15 (Spring and Summer 1975): 112–29; *Encyclopedia Judaica* 12:534–37. Menahem

G. Glenn, *Israel Salanter: Religious-Ethical Thinker* (New York: Bloch Publishing, 1953); Dov Katz, *Tenuat HaMusar* (Tel Aviv: Beitan Hasefer, 1954–67).

21. *Encyclopedia Judaica* 12:537.

22. See n. 20, above.

23. Zalman M. Schachter, "The Encounter: A Study of Counseling in Hasidism," doctoral diss., Hebrew Union College, 1968.

24. Moshe Halevi Spero, *Judaism and Psychology: Halakhic Perspectives* (New York: Ktav Publishing, 1980), 115.

25. Schachter, "The Encounter," 368.

26. Ibid., 283.

27. Ibid., 225.

28. Elie Wiesel, *Four Hasidic Masters and Their Struggle Against Melancholy* (Notre Dame, Ind.: University of Notre Dame Press, 1978), 86.

29. Schachter, "The Encounter," 315.

30. Abraham Joshua Heschel, *A Passion for Truth* (New York: Farrar, Straus & Giroux, 1973), 68.

31. Ibid.

32. Ibid., 273.

CHAPTER 4

1. Don S. Browning, *The Moral Context of Pastoral Care* (Philadelphia: Westminster Press, 1976), 129.

2. Martin Buber, *A Believing Humanism, My Testament 1902–1965*, trans. Maurice Friedman (New York: Simon & Schuster, 1967), 141–42.

3. Erich Fromm, *Psychoanalysis and Religion* (New Haven, Conn.: Yale University Press, 1950), 93.

4. Ibid., 96.

5. Erik H. Erikson, *Childhood and Society* (New York: W. W. Norton, 1957), 232.

6. Perry London, "The Rabbi as Therapist," *Moment* 5 (September 1980), last par.

7. Paul A. Schilpp and Maurice Friedman, eds., *The Philosophy of Martin Buber* (LaSalle, Ill.: Open Court Publishers, 1967), 693.

8. Michael Balint, *The Doctor, His Patient, and the Illness* (New York: International Universities Press, 1957), 216.

9. Shabbat 31a.

10. Nahum N. Glatzer, ed., *In Time and Eternity: A Jewish Reader* (New York: Schocken Books, 1946), 111.

11. Elie Wiesel, *Somewhere a Master* (New York: Summit Books, 1982), 94.

12. Franz Kobler, ed., *A Treasury of Jewish Letters* (New York: East and West Library, 1952), 1:192–93.

13. James E. Dittes, *When the People Say No: Conflict and Call to Ministry* (New York: Harper & Row, 1979), 26.

CHAPTER 5

1. Heinz Kohut, "Introspection, Empathy, and Mental Health," *International Journal of Psycho-Analysis* 63 (1982): 405.

2. Alistair V. Campbell, *Rediscovering Pastoral Care* (Philadelphia: Westminster Press, 1981), 106.

3. Ibid., 105–6.

4. Ibid., 67.

5. David Hartman, *Joy and Responsibility* (Jerusalem: Ben-Zvi-Posner, 1978), 11.

6. Ethics of the Fathers 6:6.

7. Avoth de Rabbi Nathan 8:3.

8. Makkot 10a.

9. Campbell, *Rediscovering Pastoral Care,* 17.

10. Sigmund Freud, "Lines of Advance in Psychoanalytic Theory," *The Complete Psychological Works: Standard Edition,* ed. and trans. James Strachey (New York: W. W. Norton, 1938), 17:167–68.

11. Oral communication from Rabbi Jerome Malino of Danbury, Conn., in November 1982.

Bibliography

Adler, Leon M. "From Congregation to Caring Community." *Reform Judaism* (November 1980).

Bakan, David. *Sigmund Freud and the Jewish Mystical Tradition*. Princeton, N. J.: D. Van Nostrand, 1958.

Browning, Don S. *The Moral Context of Pastoral Care*. Philadelphia: Westminster Press, 1976.

Buber, Martin. *Between Man and Man*. New York: Macmillan Co., 1965.

———. *Hasidism and Modern Man*. New York: Horizon Press, 1965.

———. *I and Thou*. New York: Charles Scribner's Sons, 1958.

———. *The Knowledge of Man*. New York: Harper & Row, 1965.

Bulka, Reuven P., ed. *A Psychology and Judaism Reader*. Springfield, Ill.: Charles C. Thomas, 1982.

Campbell, Alastair V. *Rediscovering Pastoral Care*. Philadelphia: Westminster Press, 1981.

Dresner, Samuel H. *Levi Yitzchok. Portrait of a Hasidic Master*. New York: Hartmore House, 1974.

Fromm, Erich. *Psychoanalysis and Religion*. New Haven, Conn.: Yale University Press, 1950.

———. *You Shall Be as Gods*. New York: Holt, Rinehart & Winston, 1966.

Glenn, Menahem G. *Israel Salanter: Religious-Ethical Thinker*. New York: Bloch Publishing, 1953.

Goldberg, Hillel. *Israel Salanter: Text, Structure, Idea: The Ethics and Theology of an Early Psychologist of the Unconscious*. New York: Ktav Publishing, 1982.

Green, Arthur. *Tormented Master: A Life of Rabbi Nahman of Bratslav*. New York: Schocken Books, 1981.

Grollman, Earl A. *Judaism in Sigmund Freud's World*. New York: Appleton-Century-Crofts, 1966.

———, ed. *Rabbinical Counseling*. New York: Bloch Publishing, 1967.

Kadushin, Max. *Organic Thinking: A Study in Rabbinic Thought*. New York: The Jewish Theological Seminary, 1938.

———. *The Rabbinic Mind*. New York: Bloch Publishing, 1972.

Katz, Robert L. "Becoming a Friend to Myself: With a Little Help from Sigmund Freud, Erich Fromm, and Martin Buber." In *Jews in a Free Society*, ed. Edward A. Goldman. Cincinnati: Hebrew Union College Press, 1978.

———. "Counseling, Empathy, and the Rabbi." In *Rabbinical Counseling*, ed. Grollman.

———. "Empathy in Modern Psychotherapy and the Aggada." *Hebrew Union College Annual* 30 (1959): 191–215.

———. *Empathy: Its Nature and Uses*. New York: Free Press, 1963.

———. "Jewish Values and Sociopsychological Perspectives on Aging." *Pastoral Psychology* 24 (Winter 1975).

———. "Martin Buber and Psychotherapy." *Hebrew Union College Annual* 46 (1975).

———. "Psychology and Preaching." *Central Conference of American Rabbis Journal* 10 (June 1955).

———. "The Rabbi as Preacher/Counselor. A Frame of Reference." *Central Conference of American Rabbis Journal* (June 1958).

Klein, Dennis. *Jewish Origins of the Psychoanalytic Movement*. New York: Frederick A. Praeger, 1981.

Kushner, Harold S. *When Bad Things Happen to Good People*. New York: Schocken Books, 1981.

Kushner, Lawrence. *The River of Light: Spirituality, Judaism and the Evolution of Consciousness*. New York: Harper & Row, 1981.

Lane, Belden C. "Rabbinical Stories: A Primer on Theological Method." *Christian Century* (December 16, 1981).

Liebman, Joshua Loth. *Peace of Mind*. New York: Simon & Schuster, 1946.

———, ed. *Psychiatry and Religion*. Introduction by Albert A. Goldman. Boston: Beacon Press, 1948.

Linzer, Norman. *Judaism and Mental Health*. New York: Board of Jewish Education, 1978.

Noveck, Simon, ed. *Judaism and Psychiatry*. New York: National Academy for Adult Jewish Studies, 1956.

Ostow, Mortimer. *Judaism and Psychoanalysis*. New York: Ktav Publishing, 1982.

Petuchowski, Jakob J. *Our Masters Taught*. New York: Crossroad, 1982.

Rubenstein, Richard L. *The Religious Imagination: A Study in Psychoanalysis and Jewish Theology.* Indianapolis: Bobbs-Merrill, 1968.

Schachter, Zalman M. "The Encounter: A Study of Counseling in Hasidism." Doctoral diss., Hebrew Union College, 1968.

Schachter, Zalman, and Edward Hoffman. *Sparks of Light: Counseling in the Hasidic Tradition.* Boulder, Colo.: Shambhala Publications, dist. by Random House, Westminster, Md., 1983.

Schnitzer, Rabbi Jeshaia. *New Horizons for the Synagogue.* New York: Bloch Publishing, 1956.

Schulweis, Harold. "Changing Models of Synagogue and Rabbis' Role." *Central Conference of American Rabbis Yearbook, 1975.*

Spero, Moshe Halevi. *Judaism and Psychology: Halakhic Perspectives.* New York: Ktav Publishing, 1980.

Spiro, Jack D. *A Time to Mourn: Judaism and the Psychology of Bereavement.* New York: Bloch Publishing, 1968.

Urbach, Ephraim E. *The Sages: Their Concepts and Beliefs.* 2 vols. Trans. Israel Abrahams. Jerusalem: Magnes Press, 1975.

Wiesel, Elie. *Four Hasidic Masters and Their Struggle Against Melancholy.* Notre Dame, Ind., and London: University of Notre Dame Press, 1978.

———. *Somewhere a Master: Further Hasidic Portraits and Legends.* New York: Summit Books, 1982.

———. *Souls on Fire.* New York: Random House, 1972.

Zeligs, Dorothy F. *Psychoanalysis and the Bible.* New York: Bloch Publishing, 1974.